<CODING,>
ROBOTICS,
AND
[ENGINEERING]
FOR YOUNG STUDENTS

<CODING,> ROBOTICS, AND [ENGINEERING] FOR YOUNG STUDENTS

Ann Gadzikowski

PRUFROCK PRESS INC.
WACO, TEXAS

Prufrock Press Inc.
P.O. Box 8813
Waco, TX 76714-8813
Phone: (800) 998-2208
Fax: (800) 240-0333
http://www.prufrock.com

TABLE OF CONTENTS

Introduction

Creating a model of a brain out of clay, measuring the speed of a balsa glider, writing the history of Ancient Egypt in sonnet form—these are all examples of the project-based, constructivist learning that takes place in the enrichment courses at the Center for Talent Development (CTD) at Northwestern University. The CTD mission is to provide resources, assessment services, and programs for academically talented students. We begin at age 3 in our Tadpole Academy parent-child courses. For students ages 4 through grade 8, we offer a wide variety of enrichment courses on weekends and in the summer.

In 2014, an article in *The New York Times* caught the attention of CTD program coordinators. "Reading, Writing, Arithmetic, and Lately, Coding" (Richtel, 2014) described the movement to adopt computer science as a core subject area in school districts across the country, most notably in Chicago and New York. The article discussed resources, such as the "Hour of Code" tutorials developed by Code.org, that allow young children to engage in introductory computer science learning. At CTD, we saw the need and opportunity to create a scope and sequence of computer science enrichment courses that create pathways for our youngest students to follow their interests and talents in computer science and robotics beginning in Pre-K.

In the summer of 2015 we launched our "Story Code" and "Robot Stories" curriculum tracks, eight one-week courses for grades Pre-K–3. Almost 500 students participated, and the course evaluations and assessments indicated that the pilot was very successful. We ran the courses again in the summer of 2016, inviting an interdisciplinary team of researchers from Northwestern University's School of Communication and School of Education and Social Policy to study student outcomes (Pila et al., 2016). For the summer of 2017, we created eight additional units organized into a coding track, "Coding Constructions," and a robotics track, "Robot Quest."

The challenge of creating this curriculum was that no model existed for how to teach computer science and robotics content to such young students. We began with the standalone lesson plans and activity guides that many of the robotic devices and apps provided with their products; combined these resources with what we already knew about constructivist, project-based learning; and created our own unique model that blends and balances virtual and tangible learning experiences and also provides creative challenges for advanced learners.

Another unique characteristic of our model is that the lesson plans are accessible and easy to implement by teachers with little or no background in computer science. Our priority is good teaching; we recruit instructors who have strong classroom management skills, are responsive to students, and are able to differentiate and challenge students at the appropriate level. The curriculum and resources are organized and presented using language and ideas that teachers find familiar and accessible.

During the initial development of the curriculum, we aligned our work with best practices in gifted education and developmentally appropriate practices for young children. Several resources proved to be essential, particularly from the National Association for the Education of Young Children (NAEYC), the Fred Rogers Center for Early Learning, and the Erikson Institute's Technology in Early Childhood (TEC) Center. The NAEYC position statement *Technology and Interactive Media as Tools in Early Childhood Programs Serving Children From Birth Through Age 8* (2012) inspired and empowered us to create a rich variety of learning experiences that involve tangible materials, social interaction, and play.

In October of 2016, after our Tech Beginnings curriculum had already been implemented for two summers, the K–12 Computer Science (CS) Framework was released. The framework was developed through a collaboration of key technology education organizations, such as the Computer Science Teachers Association, the National Math and Science Initiative, and Code.org. The K–12 CS Framework provides conceptual guidelines to inform the development of computer science standards and curriculum and build capacity for teaching computer science.

At CTD, we were gratified to see that the concepts and principles we used to create our curriculum aligned with the framework (K–12 Computer Science Framework Steering Committee, 2016). For example, the framework presented five "powerful ideas" that are relevant and significant in computer science learning at the early childhood level—play, patterns, problem solving, representation, and sequencing. The framework authors stated that when these five powerful ideas are applied to computer science, learning becomes "a natural extension of children's everyday engagement with their environment and builds on what educators already do in their daily practice" (p. 185).

The Tech Beginnings curriculum is aligned with all five of the essential ideas outlined in the K–12 CS Framework. In particular, the idea of representation plays a significant role in differentiation for academically talented and creative students. Our experience in other subject areas is that students' learning deepens and their thinking becomes more complex when they have the opportunity to represent their thinking in more than one way. For example, a kindergarten-level student in the CTD "Blocks and Blueprints" course learns introductory geometry concepts through 3-D construction with wooden unit blocks. The student's learning deepens when the student is challenged to represent her structure using a different medium, such as sculpting clay, sketching on paper, or casting shadows on a wall. The Tech Beginnings curriculum emphasizes this kind of multimedia and cross-media learning, with an emphasis on the importance of connecting students' learning experiences in a virtual environment with meaningful and tangible experiences in real life.

Tech Beginnings Curriculum Overview

The Tech Beginnings curriculum is organized into tracks. Each track includes four courses or units. Each summer we offer two separate tracks of tech courses: a coding track and a robotics track. At CTD, each course/unit is implemented as a one-week summer enrichment course, offered 5 days in a single week, for 3 hours each day. Thus, the lesson plans for each course/unit included in this book are designed to cover 15 hours of instruction. These lessons can be adapted to use in a weekly or biweekly enrichment experience. For example, each 3-hour session could be divided into two 90-minute sessions. Each activity or learning center described in the lessons can also be used as a standalone activity or choice in a general classroom.

Each course/unit was created to serve a mixed-age classroom. CTD enrichment courses are usually organized into grade bands that cover two grade levels: Pre-K and kindergarten, kindergarten and first grade, first and second grade, second and third grade. This model allows for a broad range of interests and abilities in each classroom. The units in this book cover Pre-K through second grade, with built-in opportunities to scaffold activities for third and even fourth grade. The curriculum is structured to allow for constant differentiation; except for the group gatherings at the beginning and end of each class, all students are rarely engaged in the same activity at the same time. The learning center structure provides students many opportunities for choice. Each center activity is designed to accommodate four to six students. Instructors also have the opportunity of assigning students to specific centers and managing the center rotation to expose students to the activities in which they most need and want to engage.

The target population for these courses is academically talented students. At CTD, the requirements for admission in most enrichment courses are academic test scores that demonstrate achievement or ability in the 90th percentile or above. Many of the Tech Beginnings concepts are one or more grade levels above a general curriculum. For a general population of mixed ability, use the lessons at a lower grade band. For example, the units at the K–1 level are probably most appropriate for a general second-grade classroom.

Each unit is organized into a structure that includes the following components:

1. track description,
2. course description,
3. essential questions,
4. learning objectives,
5. lesson plans at a glance,
6. lesson details,
7. course-specific teacher preparation,
8. ideas for differentiation, and
9. course-specific resources (if applicable).

Following the lesson plans you will find additional sections on the following topics:

> teacher preparation,
> assessment practices,
> materials and equipment, and
> resources.

When preparing to implement a Tech Beginnings unit, read through the lesson plans first to get a general idea of how the unit is organized and what content the unit covers. Then, read the section on teacher preparation and consider which training or professional tasks you will need to complete in order to feel confident in leading the unit. For example, a teacher who is new to coding may choose to complete an "Hour of Code" tutorial online (many are available at https://code.org/learn) to become more familiar with coding concepts, or a teacher who is new to robotics may want to read the teacher guide or manual for the robotic devices that will be used in the classroom. If your school does not yet own the devices described in the lesson plans, check the Materials and Equipment section for resources and recommendations related to the purchase and use of the tech devices.

Before and during the implementation of the Tech Beginnings units, use the "Lesson Plans at a Glance" charts for easy access to the schedule and sequence of activities. The Assessment section (p. 151) includes the pre- and postassessment handouts. Finally, for additional resources and suggested picture books, consult the Resources section at the end of the book.

A Note About Block and Construction Centers

When these courses were first piloted, one of the most exciting discoveries was seeing how well the block and construction play supported and complemented students' coding activities on the tablets. Even when students were not given specific instructions, their block play seemed to naturally extend and build upon what they were learning about sequences, looping, and patterns. For example, after learning the repeat or loop commands on an iPad, a child built a "rainbow wall" out of colored blocks, demonstrating a repeating "loop" of a pattern of colors across her structure.

Instructors are encouraged to use block play as an opportunity to initiate spontaneous conversations about course concepts without directing students to build or play in a certain way. Let the play and construction develop and then make objective and specific observations: "I see you have made a pattern using triangles and squares." Ask open-ended questions that encourage critical thinking and metacognition: "Tell me how you made that. How did you decide which shapes to use?"

Whenever possible, draw students' attention to the ways their block play parallels or connects to the coding concepts: "I see you made a ramp that goes up and down. That reminds me of the way Daisy goes up and down when you program her with the jump command."

A Note About Expo

In CTD enrichment courses, parents and family members are invited to visit the classroom at the end of the course. This event, which we call *Expo*, usually lasts only 15–20 minutes, but we highly recommend providing this type of opportunity for students to demonstrate and reflect upon their work and for parents to learn more about their children's experiences in coding and robotics. Parents are usually very impressed to see how even very young children can begin learning significant computer science and robotics concepts. The at-a-glance charts in each unit demonstrate how Expo can be integrated into the courses. During an Expo event, the instructor welcomes parents with a brief overview and then students are invited to guide their parents through the learning centers.

TRACK I
Coding Constructions

TRACK DESCRIPTION

The foundational concepts of computer science can be taught with a balanced variety of both virtual and tangible tools, by using apps and devices to introduce core concepts, such as patterns and sequencing, while limiting screen time to short lessons. The four Coding Constructions units provide a variety of collaborative and creative construction projects that invite young students to expand upon what they learn on their screens and bring those ideas into the real world, using blocks, clay, LEGOs, cardboard, and other three-dimensional (3-D), tangible tools. When students are challenged to take what they learn in one domain and represent those concepts in another domain using new tools and language, their work becomes more complex, detailed, and creative. The varied instructional methods employed in the Coding Constructions courses are informed by the constructionist framework developed by Seymour Papert (1993) at the Massachusetts Institute of Technology. Papert's groundbreaking work, influenced by the learning theories of Jean Piaget, emphasizes building mathematical and computer science knowledge through active engagement in a problem-solving process that is meaningful and relevant to children's lives (pp. 156–166).

The four units are:

Coding Paths and Patterns: Grades Pre-K–K

Students learn introductory coding concepts using apps, such as Kodable and Daisy the Dinosaur. Students also use tangible blocks and puzzles to construct 3-D roads, paths, and patterns that demonstrate virtual coding concepts.

Coding Levels and Layers: Grades K-1

Students learn basic coding concepts with ScratchJr, Lightbot, and Toca Builders. Students work in virtual environments using a tablet and touchscreens, then practice and expand what they've learned using 3-D construction materials, such as wood, foam, and cardboard. Students develop new levels and layers of computer science skills as they build increasingly complex structures and stories.

Learn to Code: Loops!: Grades 1-2

A *loop* is an essential coding concept prevalent in all programming languages. In this course, students use introductory coding apps like ScratchJr to learn how to create loops and other foundational coding strategies. They then deepen and extend their understanding of algorithms by using LEGOs and other 3-D construction tools to create tangible representations of virtual concepts.

Coding Scavenger Hunt: Grade 2

Introductory coding apps like ScratchJr and Hopscotch teach beginning computer science skills, as well as introduce more advanced concepts, such as *conditions* and *events*. In this course, students work at their own pace to create digital games and stories that incorporate a variety of coding strategies and algorithms. Students also practice and expand new skills through 3-D construction projects and games that demonstrate and extend coding concepts.

UNIT I
Coding Paths and Patterns

COURSE DESCRIPTION

Students learn introductory coding concepts using apps, such as Kodable and Daisy the Dinosaur. Students also use tangible blocks and puzzles to construct 3-D roads, paths, and patterns that demonstrate virtual coding concepts.

Essential Questions

> What is code?
> How do we tell computers what to do?
> What can we learn about computers and coding through play and pretending?
> How is building a path or pattern in a computer program different from building a path or pattern in real life? How is it the same?

Learning Outcomes

During the course, students will:
> learn and discuss how computers and electronic devices are controlled by code written by programmers;
> define and use computer programming terms and concepts such as *code, coding, command, programming, block, symbol, pattern, algorithm,* and *sequence;*
> write computer code using block programming apps; and
> create two- and three-dimensional paths and patterns using a variety of tools, including paper and pencil, blocks, and puzzles.

Materials

> Teacher's copies of read-aloud books (see Welcome Circle)
> 4–6 iPads with Daisy the Dinosaur and Kodable apps

> Student copies of Coding Preassessment and Coding Postassessment (see pp. 154–155)
> Pattern blocks
> Unit blocks and toy dinosaurs
> Blue painter's tape (for making a grid on the floor)
> SmartGames Dinosaurs: Mystic Islands
> Ravensburger Rivers, Roads and Rails
> Projector or 4–6 flashlights
> Clay, pom poms, cotton balls, and googly eyes
> 4–6 Etch A Sketches
> Graph paper, rulers, pencils, and markers
> Stencils and/or rubber stamps

LESSON PLANS AT A GLANCE

Monday	Tuesday	Wednesday	Thursday	Friday
Welcome Circle: Introductions and read *Everyone Can Learn to Ride a Bicycle.*	**Welcome Circle:** Read and act out *Dinosaur Dance!*	**Welcome Circle:** Read *A Fish Out of Water.*	**Welcome Circle:** Read and act out *Hare and Tortoise.*	**Welcome Circle:** Revisit *Everyone Can Learn to Ride a Bicycle.*
Mini-Lesson: Introduce the Daisy app and the *move* block.	**Mini-Lesson:** Introduce concept of loop with *repeat* block.	**Mini-Lesson:** Introduce *grow* and *shrink* blocks.	**Mini-Lesson:** Introduce if/then conditions.	**Centers:** 1. Tablets 2. Postassessment 3. Blocks and dinosaurs 4. Pattern blocks 5. Draw/write a story or map
Centers: 1. Tablets 2. Preassessment 3. Pattern blocks 4. Blocks and dinosaurs	**Centers:** 1. Tablets 2. Play Dinosaurs: Mystic Islands 3. Draw/write a story or map 4. Blocks and dinosaurs	**Centers:** 1. Tablets 2. Make dinosaur shadows grow and shrink 3. Pattern blocks 4. Play Rivers, Roads and Rails	**Centers:** 1. Tablets 2. Make a Kodable creature 3. Etch A Sketch 4. Blocks and dinosaurs 5. Mapping center	**Recess/Break**
Recess/Break	**Recess/Break**	**Recess/Break**	**Recess/Break**	**Prepare for Expo:** Create a map, code, or algorithm that the parents must follow when they arrive.
Revisit Centers	**Mini-Lesson:** Introduce concept of "troubleshooting."	**Mini-Lesson:** Introduce Kodable.	**Revisit Centers**	**Expo:** Display student work in centers; students teach parents how to use apps.
Plus: Pretend you're Daisy on a big grid.	**Revisit Centers**	**Revisit Centers**	**Plus:** Make a Kodable path on graph paper.	
Closing Circle: What is coding?	**Plus:** Add commands to blocks.	**Plus:** Kodable.	**Closing Circle:** How are iPads and Etch A Sketches the same? How are they different (Venn diagram)?	
	Closing Circle: What is a pattern?	**Closing Circle:** Compare Daisy to Kodable.		

LESSON DETAILS

Welcome Circle and Closing Circle

Welcome circle. Starting each class session with a welcome circle provides an opportunity to establish a sense of community, review the schedule and expectations, and take attendance. Students sit on the floor while the instructor leads the discussion. The instructor concludes the welcome circle with a read aloud of a storybook related to course concepts. Suggested books include:

> *Everyone Can Learn to Ride a Bicycle* **by Chris Raschka:** This book is about how we learn something new and challenging. The content of the story is not directly related to coding, but the child who is learning to ride a bike demonstrates many of the positive behaviors that have been associated with successful STEM learning, such as observing role models and trying different tools and supports (training wheels). Most of all, the book is about not giving up, even when the task seems very difficult to master. Use this book to stimulate discussion about the challenge of learning something new, and then relate that to learning to code. Revisit the book on the last day of class to review the learning and growth the class demonstrated over the course of the week.

> *Dinosaur Dance!* **by Sandra Boynton:** This silly book relates to the motion blocks used in the Daisy app. Students will enjoy acting out the movements in the book. Help students make connections between the actions in the book and the motion commands in the coding app.

> *A Fish Out of Water* **by Helen Palmer:** This classic picture book tells the story of a pet fish that won't stop growing. Students will enjoy making connections between the way the fish grows in the story and the way Daisy grows in the app. The story may also generate discussions about troubleshooting and the strategies we use to solve problems.

> *Hare and Tortoise* **by Alison Murray:** This 2016 update to the old Aesop fable includes some wonderful illustrations that demonstrate mapping concepts and spatial relationships. Discuss paths and maps in illustrations during the welcome circle and leave the book out during center time. Encourage students to draw their own maps, as inspired by the picture book or the Kodable game board. The story also demonstrates if/then conditions: *If* you are a hare, *then* you go fast and take a nap. *If* you are a tortoise, *then* you go slow and steady. Students may enjoy acting out the story of the Hare and Tortoise, taking turns playing the two contrasting roles.

Closing circle. Use the closing circle time to encourage reflection and meta-cognition about what students learned and how they learned it. The at-a-glance schedule includes suggested questions to spark discussion. You may also choose to reread the storybook from the opening circle time.

Mini-Lessons

See "Teaching Daisy/Teaching Coding" in the Teacher Preparation section (p. 16) for information about how to introduce the apps and teach specific concepts. Any large-group lessons should be brief. Students will have the opportunity to practice the concepts on tablets in learning centers.

Centers

Tablets. Students' screen time will be primarily limited to small-group work in centers of four to six students. This is the time to learn and practice the specific coding concepts that the instructor has introduced in a mini-lesson. The instructor or another adult should closely supervise this center. Students will likely need assistance, especially in the first part of the week when they are new to the apps. The other centers have been planned to reduce the need for direct supervision in order to allow the instructor to focus on students with tablets.

Pre- and postassessment. The pre- and postassessments are intended to measure and document students' general understanding of what we can do with tablets and computers. Both assessments are handouts (see pp. 154–155) that ask students to draw a picture and explain it. Many students may not yet be able to write independently. These students may dictate responses to an adult. In practice, it may be difficult to find classroom time for every student to dictate a response. Instructors should try to collect as many responses as is reasonable in the time available. Another option might be to ask parents to write down students' postassessment responses at home or during Expo.

Pattern blocks. The pattern blocks demonstrate two primary attributes or variables: shape and color. When students are invited to play and build with the pattern blocks in an open-ended manner, their structures and creations will likely demonstrate some interesting patterns and sequences. Instructors can also make gentle suggestions about creating a path or sequence, and draw students' attention to the connections between the pattern play and the coding sequences in the Daisy and Kodable apps.

Blocks and dinosaurs. This is an open-ended play center stocked with plain unit blocks and toy dinosaurs. Students can be encouraged to build and pretend in any way they choose. This is an opportunity for students to develop and try out their own ideas for imaginary scenarios.

Pretend you're Daisy (or the Kodable creature) on a big grid. This is a dramatic play activity that could go in different directions, depending on students' ideas and interests. The purpose is to make the movements of Daisy on the screen more real and tangible to students. Create a big grid on the floor using masking tape or painter's tape. Have students move around the grid by jumping or stepping from one square to another. Use the commands from Daisy or the arrow commands from Kodable to create a sequence of commands for students to follow, or have students create an algorithm for you to follow.

Play Dinosaurs: Mystic Islands. This is a spatial reasoning game that requires the players to configure a map in which the meat-eating dinosaurs (red) are never on the same island as the plant-eating dinosaurs (green). The booklet contains prompts and challenges from a beginning level to a very challenging level. The game is intended to be played by one person at a time, but teams of 2–3 students could work together to solve the puzzles. Some young students may find this game too difficult, but the game could be an ideal tool for a child with advanced academic talents who needs a differentiated challenge. Students could also be encouraged to create their own Mystic Island maps using blocks or on paper.

Draw/write a story or map. This is an open-ended writing and drawing center stocked with a variety of supplies, such as paper, pens, markers, sticky notes, stickers, stencils, etc. Students may write or draw whatever they please, but they can be encouraged to create stories that incorporate Daisy or other dinosaur characters. If an instructor or teaching assistant is available, this center can also be a place where story dictation takes place.

Add commands to blocks. On the second or third day of class, tape labels to some of the unit blocks. The labels show the commands and colors from the Daisy app: *move, turn, jump, roll, spin* (all blue), as well as *repeat 5* and *when* (both pink). These blocks can be introduced to students' block play in a deliberate, instructional way, to parallel the coding instruction for the app, or they could be simply included in the set of blocks to see if students independently discover the parallel. Students may stack the command blocks and move the toy dinosaurs in the same ways that the block code controls Daisy on the screen.

Make dinosaur shadows grow and shrink. Holding toy dinosaurs up to a light source, such as a projector or flashlight, creates a shadow on the wall. Students can make the shadows bigger or smaller, depending on how close they hold the toy to the light source. Dinosaurs grow and shrink as a tangible representation of Daisy responding to the *grow* and *shrink* block commands in the app. Students might enjoy tracing the dinosaur shadows onto paper secured to the wall. To do this, the toy must be held still by a classmate, or placed on a surface, such as a table or shelf.

Play Rivers, Roads and Rails. This is a fun, small-group sequencing game. It can be played on the floor or on a tabletop. Students take turns adding cards to build a network of rivers, roads, and rails. The game also teaches the coding concept of conditions—if the card shows a river, then it must be connected to another river card, etc.

Make a Kodable creature (and make a Kodable path). Students can make a fuzzy creature to play with as a tangible representation of the little creature in the Kodable app. The tangible creatures are symbols that represent figures on the screen. The creatures can be constructed a number of different ways using materials such as clay, pom poms, cotton balls, and googly eyes. Students can also make Kodable paths for their creatures on large pieces of graph paper by coloring squares in patterns similar to the Kodable apps. Students may want to look at screenshots from the Kodable game to get ideas for their paths.

Etch A Sketch. This classic toy presents several interesting parallels to the Daisy app. The toy can be shaken to create a cause-and-effect situation that is similar to the "when" conditional command in the Daisy app. Also, the navigation of the "cursor" on the Etch A Sketch screen requires some troubleshooting and spatial navigation skills that are similar to programming Daisy.

Mapping. Offer the same materials as the drawing/writing center, but be sure to include graph paper, rulers, and rubber stamps that can be used for creating maps.

TEACHER PREPARATION

Teaching Daisy/Teaching Coding

The Daisy app, as well as the Kodable game and any other tablet apps, can be introduced to students in a large group by projecting the iPad screen using a classroom SmartBoard or other projection device.

The command blocks in Daisy the Dinosaur are labeled with text such as "move" or "jump" rather than icons or arrows. This presents an initial challenge for young students who are not yet readers. Yet, surprisingly, our experience using this app with prereaders has been very positive. Students learn what the blocks can do through a variety of methods, through trial and error as well as by using or developing whatever sight letters or sight words they are able to learn at this point. Instructors are encouraged to create and post a key to the text blocks, where each word is represented by a corresponding symbol or icon (e.g., move = →).

Suggested sequence of instruction:

1. **Use "Challenge Mode" to introduce concepts.** In the Daisy the Dinosaur app, the Challenge Mode takes the user through a step-by-step

sequence to learn to use each command. The instructions appear as text, and most Pre-K–K students will probably not be able to work through the Challenge Mode independently. Each Challenge Mode step or task can be introduced to students using a projector or SmartBoard. The first time students use Daisy, they may also need instruction in how to use the menu and the play buttons.

2. **Teach *move* and *jump* commands.** These are the first two commands. They allow the user to move Daisy horizontally and vertically.

3. **Teach *repeat* command and the concept of loop.** The *repeat* command in Daisy introduces the concept of loop or looping in computer programming. Use the word *loop* and explain that in coding, looping is used to make a computer do the same thing over and over again. A human being might get tired or bored from looping, but computers can loop forever without tiring.

4. **Introduce troubleshooting.** Learning to solve problems and fix mistakes, or *troubleshooting*, is a very important part of computer programming. Celebrate mistakes as opportunities to learn more about how the app works and how to write code. Demonstrate making mistakes, and ask students to help you figure out what went wrong. Make a list of all of the great ways students solve problems when things don't go as expected.

5. **Teach *grow* and *shrink* commands.** The *grow* and *shrink* commands may be especially interesting to students because they demonstrate concepts of measurement and scale, and the two commands function in relation to each other. It is also possible to grow Daisy until she becomes so large she can no longer be seen on the screen. Ask students questions to spark complex and critical thinking: How much does Daisy grow each time we use the *grow* command? How could we measure that? How much does she shrink? If we make her grow three times and shrink two times, will she be bigger or smaller than when she started?

6. **Teach *when* (conditions).** The concept of *conditions* is very important in computer coding. Conditions are often expressed as *if/then* relationships. In the Daisy app, the concept of conditions is introduced using a simple *when* command that has only two options for conditions—shake or touch. One common mistake students make at this point is that they forget to touch the "play" button before they start shaking or touching. This common mistake is another opportunity for troubleshooting. Don't tell students what they've done wrong; let them try to figure it out. Although *shake* is listed first, encourage students to also use the *touch* condition; this is more similar to the conditions usually found on a tablet app with a touchscreen. Also, make sure students are gentle and careful when they shake the tablets.

IDEAS FOR DIFFERENTIATION

The structure of the lessons, with opportunities to explore a variety of learning centers, is designed to allow students to learn and explore at their own pace. Students who need more time to master new ideas can be allowed to spend a longer amount of time in a learning center, or be allowed to make their own choice for which center to visit, as long as that strategy does not disrupt the rest of the classroom.

For students needing greater challenge, here are some suggestions:

> **More challenging apps and games:** Students who are already familiar with Daisy or who are able to move through the Challenge Mode lessons very quickly may need more challenging apps to use. Kodable is a good next step after Daisy, and many students may enjoy using this app. There are also some great games for young students available at Code.org (see Resources section).

> **Challenge students to "break" the app:** Students who say or show that the Daisy app is too easy or simple can be encouraged to "break" the app. "Breaking" the app means testing, analyzing, and documenting its limits in a systematic way. How many commands can the user fit into one program? What happens when Daisy grows too large to fit on the screen? Have students make a list of the limitations and brainstorm ideas for changes and additions they would make if they were programmers. Have them write or dictate a letter to the Daisy developers (at Hopscotch Technologies, hello@gethopscotch.com) and share their feedback.

> **Add challenge to mapping activities:** For students who demonstrate a deeper interest or talent in spatial reasoning, you can provide increasingly more difficult challenges in the drawing/writing/mapping center. Provide additional measuring tools like a compass or a protractor, as well as examples of actual maps printed from the Internet or, if available, found in an atlas. Invite students to make a map of Daisy's world from the Daisy the Dinosaur app, the Kodable world in the Kodable app, the classroom or school, or any place they imagine.

> **Add challenge to the block activities:** Students with advanced academic talent in nonverbal reasoning and mathematics may enjoy the challenge of inventing their own programming language using the blocks, toys, and tools available in the classroom. Challenge students to create their own system of symbols or code to represent a simple message, such as "Please come here" or "Do you want to be my friend?" or "Happy birthday." Ask: How could you use blocks or shapes to represent that message? Could you tell a whole story using blocks?

UNIT II
Coding Levels and Layers

COURSE DESCRIPTION

Students will learn basic coding concepts with ScratchJr, Lightbot, and Toca Builders. Students will work in virtual environments using tablets and touch-screens, then practice and expand what they've learned using 3-D construction materials, such as wood, foam, and cardboard. Students develop computer science skills as they build increasingly complex structures and stories.

Essential Questions

> What do computer programmers do?
> How is writing computer code similar to building a house? How is it different?
> What does building with blocks teach us about computer science?

Learning Outcomes

During the course, students will:
> learn and discuss how computer programmers write code to make computers do certain things;
> define and use computer programming terms and concepts, such as *coding*, *sequence*, *algorithm*, and *troubleshooting*;
> practice writing block code using ScratchJr and other apps;
> build structures using 3-D construction materials that are inspired by the virtual stories and structures students create on tablets; and
> compare the ways we build code to the ways we build tangible structures, discussing, in particular, the similarities and differences between the way a physical structure has multiple levels or layers and a digital virtual environment is created by building levels or layers of code.

Materials

> Teacher's copies of read-aloud books (see Welcome Circle)
> 4–6 iPads with Lighbot (Hour of Code version), ScratchJr, and Toca Builders apps
> Student copies of Coding Preassessment and Coding Postassessment (see pp. 154–155)
> Q-BA-MAZE
> Blokus
> Robot Turtles
> Straws and Connectors
> Magna-Tiles
> LEGOs
> Pipe and Joint Construction Set
> Wooden or foam cube blocks
> Paper, pencils, and markers
> Stencils and/or rubber stamps

LESSON PLANS AT A GLANCE

Monday	Tuesday	Wednesday	Thursday	Friday
Welcome Circle: Read *Sam and Dave Dig a Hole.*	**Welcome Circle:** Read *Go Away, Big Green Monster!*	**Welcome Circle:** Read *Harold and the Purple Crayon.*	**Welcome Circle:** Read *The Dark.*	**Welcome Circle:** View cross-section picture books.
Mini-Lesson: Introduce Lightbot.	**Mini-Lesson:** Introduce ScratchJr (choosing a character, motion blocks).	**Mini-Lesson:** ScratchJr drawing tool.	**Mini-Lesson:** Introduce Toca Builder.	**Centers:** 1. Tablets 2. Postassessment 3. Games: Student choice 4. Construction: Build a structure with levels and layers
Centers: 1. Tablets 2. Preassessment 3. Games: Q-BA-MAZE 4. Construction: Straws and Connectors	**Centers:** 1. Tablets 2. Games: Blokus 3. Drafting center 4. Construction: Magna-Tiles	**Centers:** 1. Tablets 2. Games: Robot Turtles 3. Drafting center 4. Construction: LEGOs	**Centers:** 1. Tablets 2. Games: Robot Turtles 3. Drafting center 4. Construction: Cube blocks	**Recess/Break**
Recess/Break	**Recess/Break**	**Recess/Break**	**Recess/Break**	**Prepare for Expo**
Revisit Centers: Continue Lightbot: Basics 1–8.	**Mini-Lesson:** ScratchJr, cont. (choosing a background, create new background).	**Mini-Lesson:** Troubleshooting in ScratchJr and Lightbot (share strategies for solving problems).	**Revisit Centers**	**Expo:** Display student work in centers; students teach parents how to use apps.
Closing Circle: What kind of world does Lightbot live in?	**Revisit Centers**	**Revisit Centers**	**Closing Circle:** How is Toca Builder like Lightbot? How is it different?	
	Closing Circle: How is drawing in ScratchJr the same as drawing on paper? How is it different?	**Closing Circle:** If Harold (from *Harold and the Purple Crayon*) used ScratchJr, what would he draw?		

LESSON DETAILS

Welcome Circle and Closing Circle

Welcome circle. Starting each class session with a welcome circle provides an opportunity to establish a sense of community, review the schedule and expectations, and take attendance. Students sit on the floor while the instructor leads the discussion. The instructor concludes the welcome circle with a read aloud of a storybook. Suggested books include:

> ***Sam and Dave Dig a Hole* by Mac Barnett:** Discuss: What strategies did Sam and Dave use to try to find a treasure? Were they successful? Why or why not?

> ***Go Away, Big Green Monster!* by Ed Emberley:** Discuss: How did the artist use layers in this book? Could an artist create a story like this on a computer screen? How?

> ***Harold and the Purple Crayon* by Crockett Johnson:** Discuss: If Harold used ScratchJr, what would he draw?

> ***The Dark* by Lemony Snicket:** Discuss: Think about the house in this story. How many levels are there in this house? How is learning to code like walking through a dark house?

> **Cross-section picture books:** Look at some of the cross-section or cutaway illustrations in the books suggested below. If possible, project the images on the SmartBoard or screen. Discuss: *How is a computer program like a building?*

>> *Stephen Biesty's Incredible Cross-Sections*: Biesty has illustrated many remarkable cross-section books.

>> *Look Inside* by Juan and Samuel Velasco: This book is described as "cutaway illustrations and visual storytelling." It includes architectural cutaways as well as cutaway and cross-section illustrations of plants and living things. Beware of the fanciful zombie cutaway images on pages 176–177; these may frighten some students.

>> Scholastic First Discovery Books: This series of nonfiction books, such as *Under the Ground*, incorporate transparent plastic pages that demonstrate the individual layers of many different kinds of places, machines, and living things.

>> *What Do People Do All Day?* by Richard Scarry: Pages 11–12 show a cutaway, multilevel house under construction; pages 42–43 show a cutaway, multilevel paper mill; pages 56–57 show a cutaway of a multilevel cruise ship; and page 61 shows a multilevel flour mill.

Closing circle. The closing circle at the end of class can be used to share projects that have been created or coded during the course of the class that day, or to discuss some of the big ideas and questions related to the course concepts.

Mini-Lessons

See "Teaching Lightbot," "Teaching ScratchJr," and "Teaching Toca Builders" in the Teacher Preparation section (p. 24) for information about how to introduce the apps and teach specific concepts. Any large-group instruction about the apps should be brief. Most of the direct instruction about the apps and the coding concepts should take place at the tablet center.

Centers

Tablets. Students' screen time will be primarily limited to small-group work in centers of four to six students. This is the time to learn and practice the specific coding concepts that the instructor has introduced in a mini-lesson. The instructor or another adult should closely supervise this center. Students will likely need assistance, especially in the first part of the week when they are new to the apps. The other centers have been planned to reduce the need for direct supervision in order to allow the instructor to focus on students with tablets.

Pre- and postassessment. The pre- and postassessments are intended to measure and document students' general understanding of what we can do with tablets and computers. Both assessments are handouts (see pp. 154–155) that ask students to draw a picture and explain it. If students are not independent writers, they may dictate responses to an adult. In practice, it may be difficult to find classroom time for every student to dictate a response. Instructors should try to collect as many responses as is reasonable in the time available. Another option might be to ask parents to write down students' postassessment responses at home or during Expo.

Games. This center features games that teach and reinforce the spatial reasoning, sequencing, patterns, and coding concepts that students are exploring on the tablets. The games include:

> **Q-BA-MAZE:** This is more a building set than a game. Students can build structures using interlocking cubes, then drop small marbles through the structure. To ensure that every student in each small group has a chance to participate, set a rule that students take turns selecting a cube, one at a time, until all of the cubes are distributed. Make sure students complete their structures before they are given one of the marbles to test it. Holding off on the marbles until the structure is finished challenges the

student to think through the process and make predictions about how the different cubes and levels will affect the route of the marble.

> **Blokus:** Blokus is a strategy game for 2–4 players that involves placing colored block pieces on a grid. Each new piece must touch only the corner of one of your other pieces. For more information, view the game tutorial at http://www.mattelgames.com/en-us/blokus/index.html.

> **Robot Turtles:** Robot Turtles is a board game that introduces basic coding concepts. The game instructions describe different levels of challenge, such as the Basic Game, adding the Unlockables, adding the Write Program, and adding the Function Frog. The rules suggest that someone, an adult or experienced student, serve as the Turtle Mover or facilitator. However, our experience is that students prefer to move their own game pieces.

Construction. The center should be stocked with construction tools that allow students to create structures, patterns, and sequences. In the at-a-glance schedule, a new construction tool is introduced each day, but instructors should feel free to rotate and combine materials based on student interest. Construction sets include:

> Straws and Connectors,
> Magna-Tiles,
> LEGOs,
> pipes, and
> cube blocks.

Small animal and people figures could also be included for variety. Students can be encouraged to build and pretend in any way they choose. This is an opportunity for students to develop and try out their own ideas. The instructors' conversations with students and their facilitation of play should help students make connections between the virtual worlds they are creating on the screen and the real, tangible worlds they are creating in the blocks center. For example, if students use Toca Builders to build a virtual landscape, they can also be invited to recreate the same landscape in the blocks center using wooden blocks or cubes.

Drafting. This center should always be well stocked with paper, pencils, and markers. Supplemental materials such as stencils and rubber stamps can be added at various times during the week to add variety and novelty. Students can be encouraged to use their time at this center to create maps and images that represent the codes, images, and animations they are creating in Lightbot, ScratchJr, and Toca Builders.

TEACHER PREPARATION

Teaching Lightbot

This course uses the free "Hour of Code" version of Lightbot. The free app provides eight basic challenges, six procedure (function) challenges, and six loop challenges. Background information about Lightbot for teachers and parents is available at http://lightbot.com/hoclearn.html. The solutions to the Hour of Code Lightbot coding puzzles are available at http://runthrough.net/lightbot-code-hour-walkthrough.

Teaching ScratchJr

When students open the app for the first time, they will see the ScratchJr kitten and two icons: a home and a question mark. Select the question mark and view a short demonstration video. A small hand icon moves around the screen demonstrating various commands and options. The video moves very quickly and covers a lot of ground. Students will likely want to revisit this video frequently in order to learn about new commands and techniques.

After viewing the video, direct students to select the home icon. This will take them to the home screen where they can begin their first projects. The first task will be to make the ScratchJr kitten (AKA Scratch Cat Jr) move using the blue motion blocks. Some students may prefer to learn through trial and error, others may want an adult to demonstrate and teach them what to do, and others may need a combination of the two approaches.

The Official ScratchJr Book by Marina Umaschi Bers and Mitchel Resnick is very clearly written and well organized. Pages 9–12 in *The Official ScratchJr Book* provide step-by-step guidance for orienting students to motion blocks, as well as the green start flag. Pages 28–31 provide additional guidance and instruction for learning to make a character move. Instructors may prefer to use the "Animated Genres" curriculum available at: https://www.scratchjr.org/curricula/animated genres/full.pdf. The scope and sequence is very similar in both resources, but we've found that the book is a bit more user-friendly.

Teaching Toca Builders

Toca Builders is a world-building app similar to Minecraft but tailored for a younger audience. The app allows students to build a virtual world out of cube blocks by programming a group of robots, each with a unique structure and ability, to move and build. Introductory information about Toca Builders is available at https://tocaboca.com/app/toca-builders. This is a commercial app and, at this time, there is no curriculum written specifically for teaching this app. The app provides students the experience of building a structure in a virtual environment and then the challenge of trying to create a similar structure in a real, tangible environment. Each time students navigate the transition from virtual to real or back again they will likely gain new insights and ideas.

IDEAS FOR DIFFERENTIATION

The structure of the lessons, with opportunities to explore a variety of learning centers, is designed to allow students to learn and explore at their own pace. Students who need more time to master new ideas can be allowed to spend a longer amount of time in a learning center, or be allowed to make their own choice for which center to visit, as long as that strategy does not disrupt the rest of the classroom.

For students needing greater challenge, here are some suggestions:

> **Add challenge to coding activities:** Most K–1 students will find the "basic" Lightbot puzzles very challenging, especially puzzles 4–8. If a student progresses through all of the basic puzzles, he or she can go on to the "procedure" puzzles and the "looping" puzzles. Use the ideas and resources available in *The Official ScratchJr Book* to challenge students to explore additional blocks and features in ScratchJr.

> **Add challenge to mapping activities:** For students who demonstrate a deeper interest or talent in spatial reasoning, you can provide increasingly more difficult challenges in the drawing/writing/mapping center. Provide additional measuring tools like a compass or a protractor, as well as examples of actual maps printed from the Internet or, if available, found in an atlas. Invite students to make a map of Harold's world from *Harold and the Purple Crayon* or another storybook. Students could also create a map of the classroom or school, or any place they imagine.

> **Add challenge to the block activities:** Students with advanced academic talent in nonverbal reasoning and mathematics may enjoy the challenge of inventing their own programming language using the blocks, toys, and tools available in the classroom. Challenge students to create their own system of symbols or code to represent a simple message, such as "Please come here" or "Do you want to be my friend?" or "Happy birthday." Ask: How could you use blocks or shapes to represent that message? Could you tell a whole story using blocks? You could also challenge students to use the blocks and construction tools to create representations of the images and ideas represented in the apps and in the

storybooks. Could they build a block structure that represents the tunnel Dave and Sam dug in *Sam and Dave Dig a Hole*? Could they build a house out of blocks that represents the house in the storybook *The Dark*?

UNIT III
Learn to Code: Loops!

COURSE DESCRIPTION

A *loop* is an essential coding concept in all programming languages. In this course, students use introductory coding apps like ScratchJr to learn how to create loops and other foundational coding strategies. Students deepen and extend their understanding of algorithms by using LEGOs and other 3-D construction tools to create tangible representations of virtual concepts.

Essential Questions

> How do computer programmers create algorithms?
> What are loops?
> What do we learn about coding when we build 3-D models?

Learning Outcomes

During the course, students will:
> define *code*, *loop*, and *algorithm* in the context of computer programming;
> describe and demonstrate how to create a sequence of block code in ScratchJr;
> create animated projects by writing block code in ScratchJr and/or other coding apps;
> create 3-D models that mirror or expand upon the coding concepts and structures created in a virtual, digital environment; and
> compare and contrast the concept of *loops* in coding and *loops* in tangible structures.

Materials

> Teacher's copies of read-aloud books (see Welcome Circle)

> 4–6 iPads with ScratchJr, Daisy the Dinosaur, and Lighbot (Hour of Code version) apps
> Student copies of Coding Preassessment and Coding Postassessment (see pp. 154–155)
> Marble run
> LEGOs
> KEVA planks
> Straws and Connectors
> Robot Turtles
> Qwirkle
> Graph paper, pencils, and markers
> Stencils, stickers, and rubber stamps
> Sticky note pads or index cards and binder clips (for flipbooks)

LESSON PLANS AT A GLANCE

Monday	Tuesday	Wednesday	Thursday	Friday
Welcome Circle: Introductions and read *Roller Coaster*. **Mini-Lesson:** Introduce ScratchJr. **Centers:** 1. Tablets: ScratchJr 2. Preassessment 3. Marble run 4. Construction: LEGOs **Recess/Break** **Revisit Centers** **Closing Circle:** What do you like about ScratchJr? How is coding in ScratchJr different from playing a computer game?	**Welcome Circle:** Read *Round Trip*. **Mini-Lesson:** Focus on repeat block in ScratchJr. **Centers:** 1. Tablets: ScratchJr 2. Games: Robot Turtles 3. Drafting center: Flipbooks 4. Construction: KEVA planks **Recess/Break** **Revisit Centers** **Closing Circle:** How is computer animation (such as coding in ScratchJr) different from hand animation in a flipbook? How is it the same?	**Welcome Circle:** Read *Zephyr Takes Flight*. **Mini-Lesson:** Loops in Daisy the Dinosaur. **Centers:** 1. Tablets: ScratchJr or Daisy 2. Games: Robot Turtles 3. Drafting center: Maps and mazes 4. Construction: Straws and Connectors **Recess/Break** **Revisit Centers** **Closing Circle:** How is playing Robot Turtles similar to coding in ScratchJr? How is it different?	**Welcome Circle:** Read *Green Eggs and Ham*. **Mini-Lesson:** Loops in Lightbot. **Centers:** 1. Tablets: ScratchJr or Lightbot 2. Games: Qwirkle 3. Marble run 4. Construction: Student choice **Recess/Break** **Revisit Centers** **Closing Circle:** How has learning to code in ScratchJr (and the other apps) changed the way you think about computers? Is coding easier or harder than you expected? What else do you want to learn about computers and computer science?	**Welcome Circle:** Revisit *Roller Coaster*. **Centers:** 1. Tablets: Student choice 2. Postassessment 3. Games: Qwirkle 4. Drafting center: Student choice **Recess/Break** **Prepare for Expo** **Expo:** Display student work; students teach parents how to use apps.

LESSON DETAILS

Welcome Circle and Closing Circle

Starting each class session with a welcome circle provides an opportunity to establish a sense of community, review the schedule and expectations, and take attendance. Students sit on the floor while the instructor leads the discussion. The instructor concludes the welcome circle with a read aloud of a storybook. The closing circle at the end of the class can be used to discuss and reflect on the events of the day. Suggested books include:

> *Roller Coaster* **by Marla Frazee:** Discuss: How is riding a roller coaster like learning to code? Revisit this question on the last day of class. Point out the loop illustration and the words in the text: "And goes all-l-l-l-l-l-l the way around." Ask: What else can make a loop? Can a string make a loop? Can a line make a loop? Can a bird or an animal make a loop? Can words and letters make a loop? Can computer code make a loop?

> *Round Trip* **by Ann Jonas:** Read the story from beginning to end, and then flip the book over to read from the end to the beginning. Discuss: How is a round trip like a loop? Is it possible to animate a story like this in ScratchJr? Why or why not?

> *Zephyr Takes Flight* **by Steve Light:** Discuss: How does an airplane make a loop? How is an airplane loop like a loop command in code? How is it different? At recess, if the class goes outdoors, invite students to make paper airplanes and try to fly them in a loop.

> *Green Eggs and Ham* **by Dr. Seuss:** Discuss: How could you animate this story in ScratchJr? When and how would you use the loop/repeat blocks?

Mini-Lessons

See "Teaching ScratchJr," "Teaching Daisy the Dinosaur," and "Teaching Lightbot" in the Teacher Preparation section (p. 31) for information about how to introduce the apps and teach specific concepts. Any large-group instruction about the apps should be brief. Most of the direct instruction about the apps and the coding concepts should take place at the tablet center.

Centers

Tablets. Students' screen time will be primarily limited to small-group work in centers of four to six students. This is the time to learn and practice the specific coding concepts that the instructor has introduced in a mini-lesson. The instructor or another adult should closely supervise this center. Students will likely need assistance, especially in the first part of the week when they are new to the apps. The other centers have been planned to reduce the need for direct supervision in order to allow the instructor to focus on students with tablets.

Pre- and postassessments. The pre- and postassessments are intended to measure and document students' general understanding of what we can do with tablets and computers. Both assessments are handouts (see pp. 154–155) that ask students to draw a picture and explain it. If students are not independent writers, they may dictate responses to an adult. In practice, it may be difficult to find classroom time for every student to dictate a response. Instructors should try to collect as many responses as is reasonable in the time available. Another option might be to ask parents to write down students' postassessment responses at home or during Expo.

Marble run. Marble run construction sets allow students to create a physical, tangible representation of an algorithm. Each section of the marble run tubing is like a command block in computer code. Assembling a tower of marble run pieces is like putting together a sequence of code. Challenge students to make connections between the movement blocks in ScratchJr and the shape of the marble run pieces. Some pieces are similar to the *repeat/loop* command. Others pieces are similar to the *move forward* or *jump* commands.

In terms of classroom management, instructors may choose to wait to distribute the marbles until after students have assembled their structures. This challenges students to think ahead, plan, and predict how the marble will travel through the marble run structure. If time permits, have students talk through the design and strategies of their structures before they are given a marble.

Construction. The center should be stocked with a rotating variety of materials that allow students to create structures, patterns, and shapes. The options suggested in the at-a-glance schedule include LEGOs, KEVA planks, and Straws and Connectors. Small animal and people figures, as well as cars and wheeled toys, could also be included for variety. Students should be encouraged to build and pretend in any way they choose. This is an opportunity for students to develop and try out their own ideas for imaginary scenarios and structures that may or may not be related to the coding projects. Instructors' conversations and facilitation of play should help students make connections between the virtual worlds they are creating on the screen and the real, tangible worlds they are creating in the blocks center.

Games. Robot Turtles is a board game that introduces basic coding concepts. The game instructions describe different levels of challenge, such as the Basic Game, adding the Unlockables, adding the Write Program, and adding the Function Frog. Playing the game requires an adult to serve as a facilitator. If an adult is not available to facilitate the game, other games that teach patterns and spatial reasoning, such as Qwirkle, could be offered at this learning center.

Drafting. This center should be well stocked with graph paper, pencils, and markers. Supplemental materials, such as stencils, stickers, and rubber stamps, can be added at various times during the week to add variety and novelty. The at-a-glance schedule suggests specific activities such as making flipbooks or creating maps and mazes. For the flipbooks, provide sticky note pads or index cards (secured with binder clips) for students to draw on.

TEACHER PREPARATION

Teaching ScratchJr

When students open the app for the first time, they will see the ScratchJr kitten and two icons: a home and a question mark. Select the question mark and view a short demonstration video. A small hand icon moves around the screen demonstrating various commands and options. The video moves very quickly and covers a lot of ground. Students will likely want to revisit this video frequently in order to learn about new commands and techniques.

After viewing the video, direct students to select the home icon. This will take them to the home screen where they can begin their first projects. The first task will be to make the ScratchJr kitten (AKA Scratch Cat Jr) move using the blue motion blocks. Some students may prefer to learn through trial and error, others may want an adult to demonstrate and teach them what to do, and others may need a combination of the two approaches.

The Official ScratchJr Book by Marina Umaschi Bers and Mitchel Resnick is very clearly written and wellorganized. Pages 9–12 in *The Official ScratchJr Book* provide step-by-step guidance for orienting students to motion blocks, as well as the green start flag. Pages 28–31 provide additional guidance and instruction for learning to make a character move. Instructors may prefer to use the "Animated Genres" curriculum available at: https://www.scratchjr.org/curricula/animatedgenres/full.pdf. The scope and sequence is very similar in both resources, but we've found that the book is a bit more user-friendly.

Some students may already have had some experience with ScratchJr. Students should be allowed to experiment and work independently at their own pace.

Teaching Daisy the Dinosaur

Daisy the Dinosaur is an introductory coding app used in the Pre-K–K coding courses. Students in this course may have had previous experience with the Daisy the Dinosaur app. The value of revisiting this app is to demonstrate how a *repeat* or *loop* command is represented in multiple apps. For students new to the Daisy app, use the "Challenge Mode" to introduce students to each command, including the *repeat* block. For students already familiar with the Daisy app, invite them to use the Free Play mode to show you how to use the *repeat* block to make Daisy move, grow, or shrink.

Teaching Lightbot

This course uses the free "Hour of Code" version of Lightbot. The free app provides eight basic challenges, six procedure (function) challenges, and six loop challenges. Background information about Lightbot for teachers and parents can be found here: http://lightbot.com/hoclearn.html. The solutions to the Hour of Code Lightbot coding puzzles are available at: http://runthrough.net/lightbot-code-hour-walkthrough.

IDEAS FOR DIFFERENTIATION

The structure of the lessons, with opportunities to explore a variety of learning centers, is designed to allow students to learn and explore at their own pace. Students who need more time to master new ideas can be allowed to spend a longer amount of time in a learning center, or be allowed to make their own choice for which center to visit, as long as that strategy does not disrupt the rest of the classroom.

For students needing greater challenge, here are some suggestions:

> **ScratchJr:** ScratchJr allows young students to explore a surprisingly broad variety of techniques, ideas, and projects. It is unlikely that a student would run out of ideas for ScratchJr during one week of class, even if the student has had previous experience with the app. Use the ideas and resources available in *The Official ScratchJr Book* to challenge students to explore additional blocks and features in ScratchJr.

> **Add challenge to mapping/drafting activities:** For students who demonstrate a deeper interest or talent in spatial reasoning, you can provide increasingly more difficult challenges in the drawing/writing/mapping center. Provide additional measuring tools like a compass or a protractor, as well as examples of actual maps printed from the Internet or,

if available, found in an atlas. Invite students to make a map of the tracks of the roller coaster represented in the *Roller Coaster* picture book or a map of the places represented in *Round Trip*. Students could also create a map of the classroom, school, or any place they imagine.

> **Add challenge to the block activities:** Students with advanced academic talent in nonverbal reasoning and mathematics may enjoy the challenge of inventing their own symbolic programming language or code using the blocks and tangible objects available in the classroom. For example, challenge students to use the blocks to create a line of code, like the block code in ScratchJr. Or invite them to use blocks to represent a map or road from one of the picture books. Ask: Could you tell a whole story using blocks? How would you do that?

> **Add challenge to literacy activities:** Students who are ready for a storytelling or story writing challenge can be encouraged to develop original stories on paper or using electronic resources, such as the Superhero Comic Book Maker app from Duck Duck Moose. Students who are capable or advanced writers should be encouraged to add details and dialogue to both their written work and their digital creations.

UNIT IV
Coding Scavenger Hunt

COURSE DESCRIPTION

Introductory coding apps like ScratchJr and Hopscotch teach beginning computer science skills, as well as introduce more advanced concepts, such as *conditions* and *events*. In this course, students work at their own pace to create digital games and stories that incorporate a variety of coding strategies and algorithms. Students also practice and expand new skills through 3-D construction projects and games that demonstrate and extend coding concepts. Although this course is designed for children in second grade, these lesson plans also include options for differentiation that allow for scaffolding for third graders.

Essential Questions

> How do computer programmers create games and stories?
> What can we learn from building a 3-D model of code?
> Can a game tell a story? Why or why not?

Learning Outcomes

During the course, students will:
> learn how to create a sequence of block code in ScratchJr and/or Hopscotch;
> demonstrate coding concepts such as *conditions* and *troubleshooting*;
> create characters, stories, and games through writing, drawing, 3-D construction, and coding; and
> evaluate the benefits and challenges of using coding to play digital games, as compared to playing games using tangible objects.

Materials

> Teacher's copies of read-aloud books (see Welcome Circle)
> 4–6 iPads with ScratchJr and Hopscotch apps
> Student copies of Coding Preassessment and Coding Postassessment (see pp. 154–155)
> Robot Turtles
> Code Master
> SET
> LEGOs, cube blocks, foam blocks, and Straws and Connectors
> Graph paper, pencils, and markers
> Stencils, stickers, and rubber stamps
> Game pieces, dice, etc. (for students to design their own games)

LESSON PLANS AT A GLANCE

Monday	Tuesday	Wednesday	Thursday	Friday
Welcome Circle: Introductions and read *This Is Not My Hat*.	**Welcome Circle:** Read *Jumanji*.	**Welcome Circle:** Read *Henry's Map*.	**Welcome Circle:** Read *Madlenka*.	**Welcome Circle:** Read *Hide and Snake*.
Mini-Lesson: Introduce ScratchJr.	**Mini-Lesson:** Creating games in ScratchJr.	**Mini-Lesson:** Introduce Hopscotch.	**Mini-Lesson:** Creating games in Hopscotch.	**Centers:** 1. Tablets: Student choice 2. Postassessment 3. Drafting center 4. Construction
Centers: 1. Tablets: ScratchJr 2. Preassessment 3. Games: Robot Turtles 4. Construction	**Centers:** 1. Tablets: ScratchJr 2. Games: Robot Turtles 3. Drafting center 4. Construction	**Centers:** 1. Tablets: Hopscotch 2. Games: Code Master 3. Drafting center 4. Construction	**Centers:** 1. Tablets: Hopscotch 2. Games: SET 3. Drafting center 4. Construction	**Recess/Break**
Recess/Break	**Recess/Break**	**Recess/Break**	**Recess/Break**	**Prepare for Expo**
Revisit Centers	**Revisit Centers**	**Revisit Centers**	**Revisit Centers**	**Expo:** Display student work in centers; students teach parents how to use apps and play the games.
Closing Circle: Is coding more like writing a story or more like solving a math problem?	**Closing Circle:** Does a game have to have a winner? Why or why not?	**Closing Circle:** Compare a flat map to a globe. What factors affect how a map is designed? Are maps facts or opinions?	**Closing Circle:** Is it possible to design a game that does not have a setting, such as a grid or a board?	

LESSON DETAILS

Welcome Circle and Closing Circle

Starting each class session with a welcome circle provides an opportunity to establish a sense of community, review the schedule and expectations, and take attendance. Students sit on the floor while the instructor leads the discussion. The instructor concludes the welcome circle with a read aloud of a storybook. The closing circle at the end of the class can be used to reflect on the concepts explored during the course of the day.

> *This Is Not My Hat* **by Jon Klassen:** This story can be used to introduce course concepts, such as sequencing and problem solving. The story is also related to the title of the class—Scavenger Hunt. Discuss the meaning of the word *hunt*. When is a hunt a game, and when is it something else? Learning to code involves hunting for solutions to problems. Students can also create hunting games, hidden clues, and mysterious puzzles using code.

> *Jumanji* **by Chris Van Allsburg:** This story can be used to talk about the characteristics of games. What makes a game fun and exciting?

> *Henry's Map* **by David Elliot:** This story can be used to draw students' attention to the characteristics of maps—on a piece of paper or in a book, as well as in a digital environment on a screen. The story demonstrates concepts of spatial reasoning, orientation, and perspective that can be discussed in the context of students' coding projects.

> *Madlenka* **by Peter Sís:** The illustrations in this story provide further creative explorations of concepts related to spatial relationships and mapping.

> *Hide and Snake* **by Keith Baker:** Use the illustrations in this story to challenge students to think about the ways ideas and images can be concealed or hidden in a game—on paper, in a digital environment on a screen, and in real life.

Mini-Lessons

See "Teaching ScratchJr and Hopscotch" in the Teacher Preparation section (p. 39) for information about how to introduce the apps and teach specific concepts. Any large-group instruction about the apps should be brief. Most of the direct instruction about the apps and the coding concepts should take place at the tablet center.

Centers

Tablets. Students' screen time will be primarily limited to small-group work in centers of four to six students. This is the time to learn and practice the specific coding concepts that the instructor has introduced in a mini-lesson. The instructor or another adult should closely supervise this center. Students will likely need assistance, especially in the first part of the week when they are new to the apps. The other centers have been planned to reduce the need for direct supervision in order to allow the instructor to focus on students with tablets.

Pre- and postassessments. The pre- and postassessments are intended to measure and document students' general understanding of what we can do with tablets and computers. Both assessments are handouts (see pp. 154–155) that ask students to draw a picture and explain it. If students are not independent writers, they may dictate responses to an adult. In practice, it may be difficult to find classroom time for every student to dictate a response. Instructors should try to collect as many responses as is reasonable in the time available. Another option might be to ask parents to write down students' postassessment responses at home or during Expo.

Games. Robot Turtles is a board game that introduces basic coding concepts. The game instructions describe different levels of challenge, such as the Basic Game, adding the Unlockables, adding the Write Program, and adding the Function Frog. Playing the game requires an adult to serve as a facilitator. Another game that teaches coding concepts is Code Master. The instructions describe this as a single player game, but two students could work together as partners to solve each challenge. SET is a logic card game for 1–4 players that develops computational thinking and visual perception.

Construction. Offer at least one type or set of construction materials each day. Options will vary depending on site, but may include options such as LEGOs, cube blocks, foam blocks, and Straws and Connectors. Although students should have opportunities for free play in the construction center, instructors can also encourage students to create 3-D representations of the virtual environments in the coding apps and games.

Drafting. This center should be well stocked with graph paper, pencils, and markers. Supplemental materials, such as stencils, stickers, and rubber stamps, can be added at various times during the week to add variety and novelty. Students can be encouraged to sketch or write their ideas and plans for coding projects. They can also make maps, diagrams, and flowcharts that represent the coding process.

As the week progresses and the class spends time identifying the characteristics of games, index cards and dice can also be added to encourage students to make up their own paper and cardboard games.

TEACHER PREPARATION

Teaching ScratchJr and Hopscotch

ScratchJr and Hopscotch are both excellent tools for students to use to create their own animated projects using block programming. ScratchJr allows for a great deal of variety and complexity for students to continue to learn and experiment as they create more complex backgrounds and multiple characters, add effects such as sound and dialogue, and program conditions that allow for the story to take multiple paths.

Use *The Official ScratchJr Book* or the online ScratchJr K–2 curriculum ("Animated Genres," available at https://www.scratchjr.org/teach/curricula/animated-genres) to teach ScratchJr mini-lessons. Chapter 4 in *The Official ScratchJr Book* is devoted entirely to activities that teach students how to create games.

The Hopscotch app provides three tutorial projects: Jump In, Draw With Code, and Whack-a-Mole. When a tutorial project is opened, a small box appears on the right side that provides instructions for following the tutorial. The downloadable Hopscotch Curriculum is also a valuable resource for teachers (available at http://hopscotch-curriculum-files.s3.amazonaws.com/Hopscotch_Curriculum.pdf). Both the tutorial projects and the curriculum are valuable and useful tools for teaching Hopscotch. Instructors may choose to use one or the other, or a combination of both.

Some students may already have had some experience with ScratchJr and/or Hopscotch. Students should be allowed to experiment and work independently at their own pace. The ScratchJr online curriculum resources also include project cards and Hour of Code challenges that can be used to challenge students to try new tools and coding experiences.

IDEAS FOR DIFFERENTIATION

The structure of the lessons, with opportunities to explore a variety of learning centers, is designed to allow students to learn and explore at their own pace. Students who need more time to master new ideas can be allowed to spend a longer amount of time in a learning center, or be allowed to make their own choice for which center to visit, as long as that strategy does not disrupt the rest of the classroom.

For students needing greater challenge, here are some suggestions:

> **Create a scavenger hunt:** Students who are ready for an additional challenge can be invited to create a real or virtual scavenger hunt for the class. These websites provide helpful tips and instructions:

   ▶ "How to Write Fun and Challenging Scavenger Hunt Clues" (available at http://www.scavenger-hunt-fun.com/scavenger-hunt-clues.html)

   ▶ "Scavenger Hunt Creator" (available at http://www.scavengerhunt riddles.net/scavenger-hunts/create)

> **ScratchJr and Hopscotch:** ScratchJr and Hopscotch allow young students to explore a surprisingly broad variety of techniques, ideas, and projects. It is unlikely that a student would run out of ideas during one week of class, even if the student has had previous experience with the apps. Use the ideas and resources available in *The Official ScratchJr Book* as well as the online Hopscotch Curriculum to challenge students to explore additional blocks and features in the apps.

> **Teaching coding concepts using other apps:** Students who seem interested in trying a different kind of coding experience may enjoy playing an educational coding game, such as the Cargo-Bot app or the web-based tutorials at Code.org.

> **Add challenge to mapping/drafting activities:** For students who demonstrate a deeper interest or talent in spatial reasoning, you can provide increasingly more difficult challenges in the drawing/writing/mapping center. Provide additional measuring tools like a compass or a protractor, as well as examples of actual maps printed from the Internet or, if available, found in an atlas. Use the class picture books as inspiration for student maps. For example, invite students to make 4-sided *Madlenka*-style maps of the school or their classroom.

> **Add challenge to the block activities:** Students with advanced academic talent in nonverbal reasoning and mathematics may enjoy the challenge of inventing their own symbolic programming language or code using the blocks and tangible objects available in the classroom. For example, challenge students to use the blocks to create a line of code, like the block code in ScratchJr, or invite them to use blocks to create or represent a game or story from one of the coding projects.

TRACK II
Story Code

TRACK DESCRIPTION

Authors find inspiration for stories everywhere—the people they meet, the places they visit, even from the stories told by other authors. In Story Code animation courses, students seek inspiration for their own stories through games, dramatic play, and books as they animate their creations using educational apps and computer programs. Along the way, students learn the fundamentals of coding, such as creating a sequence of commands and troubleshooting their programs for accuracy and efficiency.

The units are:

Story Code Alpha: Grades Pre-K-K

Students use touchscreens and educational apps, such as Daisy the Dinosaur and Kodable, to learn introductory programming and coding concepts, including *block*, *loop*, *symbol*, and *sequence*.

Story Code Beta: Grades K-1

Young programmers use ScratchJr, as well as traditional methods like drawing, writing, and dramatization, to bring their stories to life.

Story Code Gamma: Grades 1-2

Students use creativity and critical thinking to develop and present stories using ScratchJr as well as Hopscotch.

Story Code Delta: Grade 2

Students create detailed narratives with multiple characters and settings. They learn to animate their stories using ScratchJr and web-based Scratch.

UNIT I
Story Code Alpha

COURSE DESCRIPTION

Stories can be shared in many ways: through a book, a painting, on stage, or even through computer animation. Students use touchscreens and educational apps, such as Daisy the Dinosaur and Kodable, to learn introductory programming and coding concepts, such as *block*, *symbol*, and *sequence*.

Essential Questions

> How does a computer work?
> What characters and stories can we create on computers?
> What can we learn about computers and coding through play and pretending?

Learning Outcomes

During the course, students will:
> learn and discuss how computers and electronic devices are controlled by code written by programmers;
> define and use computer programming terms and concepts, such as *code*, *coding*, *command*, *block*, *symbol*, *sequence*, and *loop*;
> write computer code using block programming apps; and
> create stories using words, images, dramatic play, and animation apps.

Materials

> Teacher's copies of read-aloud books (see Welcome Circle)
> 4–6 iPads with the Daisy the Dinosaur and Kodable apps
> Student copies of Coding Preassessment and Coding Postassessment (see pp. 154–155)

> Dinosaur avatar templates (see Centers)
> Memory game template (see Centers)
> Toy dinosaurs and unit blocks
> Dinosaur masks, cloaks, and other props
> Paper, pencils, and other writing materials
> Stencils and/or rubber stamps
> Model Magic clay
> Shrinky Dinks kit
> Flashlights
> Cream and small jars to make butter (see Centers)
> 4–6 Etch A Sketches
> Clay, pom poms, cotton balls, googly eyes, and other craft supplies

LESSON PLANS AT A GLANCE

Monday	Tuesday	Wednesday	Thursday	Friday
Welcome Circle: Introductions and read *How Do Dinosaurs Go to School?*	**Welcome Circle:** Read *Danny and the Dinosaur* (remove or skip the museum illustration with the Indian and the guns).	**Welcome Circle:** Read *Dinosaur Roar!*	**Welcome Circle:** Read *How Do Dinosaurs Play with Their Friends?* and/or *How Do Dinosaurs Eat Their Food?*	**Welcome Circle:** Dictate class story, "How Do Dinosaurs Learn to Code?"
Centers: 1. Preassessment 2. Create a dinosaur avatar 3. Memory game mystery 4. Toy dinosaurs and blocks	**Mini-Lesson:** Introduce *loop* and *repeat* blocks.	**Mini-Lesson:** Introduce *grow* and *shrink* blocks and troubleshooting.	**Mini-Lesson:** Introduce if/then conditions, *when* block in Daisy, and colored squares in Kodable.	**Centers:** 1. Tablets 2. Illustrate class story 3. Blocks and dino toys 4. Postassessment tool
Recess/Break	**Centers:** 1. Tablets 2. Rubber stamps 3. Stack/build command blocks 4. Write/draw a story	**Centers:** 1. Tablets 2. Shrinky dinks 3. Trace dinosaur shadows 4. Write/draw a story	**Centers:** 1. Tablets 2. Make and shake butter or play with Etch A Sketch 3. Make a Kodable fuzz creature 4. Write/draw a story	**Recess/Break**
Mini-Lesson: Introduce Daisy the Dinosaur and *move* and *jump* blocks.	**Recess/Break**	**Recess/Break**		**Prepare for Expo**
Centers: 1. Tablets: Daisy the Dinosaur 2. Pretend you're Daisy 3. Stack/build command blocks 4. Draw/write a Daisy story	**Mini-Lesson:** Introduce troubleshooting.	**Mini-Lesson:** Introduce Kodable.	**Recess/Break**	**Expo:** Present class story; display student work in centers; students teach parents how to use apps.
	Revisit Centers: Change rubber stamps to Model Magic.	**Revisit Centers:** Change Shrinky Dinks to Daisy dance party.	**Revisit Centers:** Change butter activity to make a Kodable path.	
Closing Circle: Read and act out today's stories.	**Closing Circle:** Read and act out today's stories.	**Closing Circle:** Read and act out today's stories.	**Closing Circle:** Read and act out today's stories.	

LESSON DETAILS

Welcome Circle and Closing Circle

Starting each class session with a welcome circle provides an opportunity to establish a sense of community, review the schedule and expectations, and take attendance. Students sit on the floor while the instructor leads the discussion. The instructor concludes the welcome circle with a read aloud of a dinosaur-related storybook. The books are chosen to connect to the character of Daisy in the Daisy the Dinosaur animation app. In this class, the focus is on storytelling, not paleontology, so the suggested dinosaur books are fantasy stories. Like Daisy in the app, the dinosaurs in the stories function as characters or "avatars" that represent young students and other people in their lives. Suggested books include:

> ***How Do Dinosaurs Go to School?* by Jane Yolen:** This book is a delightful read aloud and particularly appropriate for the first day of a new unit. The structure of the story, written primarily in the form of questions, can be used as a model later in the unit when students are asked to respond to the prompt, "How do dinosaurs learn to code?"

> ***Danny and the Dinosaur* by Syd Hoff:** The dinosaur illustrations in this vintage children's book are drawn in a simple style that parallels the Daisy app. The story invites children to imagine what they might do if they had a dinosaur friend. Teachers are encouraged to skip the first few pages of the book which feature museum displays of Indians and weapons that most would consider inappropriate for a 21st-century classroom.

> ***Dinosaur Roar!* by Paul and Henrietta Stickland:** This playful picture book inspires students to think creatively about the dinosaur figures and characters in this unit.

> ***How Do Dinosaurs Eat Their Food?* by Jane Yolen:** This book is another variation in the Jane Yolen dinosaur series. Reading additional books in this series will help children learn and predict the patterns in the question-and-answer story structure.

> ***How Do Dinosaurs Play With Their Friends?* by Jane Yolen:** This book is yet another example from the Jane Yolen dinosaur series. This particular story, which focuses on friendships, can also help support conflict resolution and problem-solving practices in the classroom.

Mini-Lessons

See "Teaching Daisy/Teaching Coding" in the Teacher Preparation section (p. 51) for information about how to introduce the apps and teach specific concepts. Any large-group lessons should be brief. Students will have the opportunity to practice the concepts on tablets in learning centers.

Centers

Tablets. Students' screen time will be primarily limited to small-group work in centers of four to six students. This is the time to learn and practice the specific coding concepts that the instructor has introduced in a mini-lesson. The instructor or another adult should closely supervise this center. Students will likely need assistance, especially in the first part of the week when they are new to the apps. The other centers have been planned to reduce the need for direct supervision in order to allow the instructor to focus on students with tablets.

Pre- and postassessment. The pre- and postassessments are intended to measure and document students' general understanding of what we can do with tablets and computers. Both assessments are handouts (see pp. 154–155) that ask students to draw a picture and explain it. If students are not independent writers, they may dictate responses to an adult. In practice, it may be difficult to find classroom time for every student to dictate a response. Instructors should try to collect as many responses as is reasonable in the time available and are not expected to collect a response from every child. Another option might be to ask parents to write down the child's postassessment response at home or during Expo.

Create a dinosaur avatar. This activity teaches and reinforces the concept of *symbol*, that one thing can represent another thing. The words *symbol* and *avatar* should be used and defined for students in the context of this activity. The instructor can create avatar templates ahead of time (see Figure 1), and students can be invited to pick a page ("My Dinosaur Avatar") to name and color or to draw their own dinosaur, freehand or with a stencil. Students can also write or dictate words that describe their dinosaur avatar. If the templates present several different types of dinosaurs, the avatars can be used later to divide into groups or as characters in students' stories (e.g., "It's time for the brontosauruses to move to the tablet center.").

Memory game mystery. This is a conventional memory game played with cards that contain images of household items that are controlled by computer chips (integrated circuits) and code. Students should be invited to play the game without explanation. As they play, they will likely begin to notice that some of the items are similar. At the end of the game, the winner gets to open the "mystery envelope" and read (or say with the instructor's assistance) the question on the paper inside: "What do all of these things have in common?" Students can discuss the question in their small group, and if an adult is available to take notes, write down their ideas. This activity also serves as a preassessment activity. Figure 2

Figure 1. Sample dinosaur avatar page.

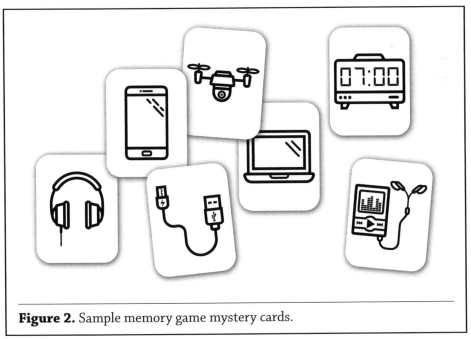

Figure 2. Sample memory game mystery cards.

is an example of mystery game cards. To make your own technology memory game, take photos of a variety of machines and devices that are common in children's households, such as a smartphone, programmable coffee maker or other household appliance, robotic toy, laptop, television and remote, car dashboard, electronic keyboard, vacuum cleaner, refrigerator, etc. Print two copies of each photo and glue them to index cards.

Toy dinosaurs and blocks. This is an open-ended play center stocked with blocks and sturdy toy dinosaurs. Students can be encouraged to build and pretend in any way they choose. This is an opportunity for students to develop and try out their own ideas for imaginary scenarios.

Pretend you're Daisy. This is a dramatic play activity that could go in different directions, depending on students' ideas and interests. The purpose of the activity is to encourage creativity and storytelling in ways that make the Daisy on the screen seem more real and tangible. Students can be invited to dress up like dinosaurs using masks, cloaks, or silly props. Students can draw or paint a mural that looks like the background in Daisy's world, or create their own fanciful background. Students could also make a path on the floor for Daisy to follow using the block commands from the app.

Stack/build command blocks. Some of the unit blocks can be labeled with the commands and colors from the Daisy app: *move*, *turn*, *jump*, *roll*, *spin* (all blue), as well as *repeat 5* and *when* (both pink). These blocks could be introduced to students' block play in a deliberate, instructional way, to parallel the coding instruction for the app, or they could be simply included in the set of blocks to see if students independently discover the parallel. Students may stack the command blocks and move the toy dinosaurs in the same ways that the block code controls Daisy on the screen.

Draw/write a Daisy story. This is an open-ended writing and drawing center stocked with a variety of supplies, such as paper, pens, markers, sticky notes, stickers, stencils, etc. Students may write or draw whatever they please, but they can be encouraged to create stories that incorporate Daisy or other dinosaur characters. If an instructor or teaching assistant is available, this center can also be a place where story dictation takes place.

Rubber stamps/rebus stories. In a rebus story, a picture represents words or letters. Reading and creating rebus stories helps reinforce the concept of symbol. It also teaches that something small can represent something bigger, just like the *repeat* or *function* concepts in computer coding. Using a rubber stamp is much easier and quicker than writing long words, in the same way that the *repeat 5* command makes coding quicker and easier in the Daisy app. The materials at this learning center will include rubber stamps, ink pads, pencils, paper, as well as some examples of rebus stories.

Model Magic. Model Magic clay is a material that can be used by students in a variety of ways. Students may create whatever they please, but they can be encouraged to create figures that represent the stories they are writing and programming in class.

Shrinky Dinks. Making Shrinky Dinks is a craft project that demonstrates, in a very tangible way, the *shrink* command in the Daisy app. Students draw on Shrinky Dinks plastic sheets with permanent markers and cut out their figures. When the plastic pieces are baked in an oven for just a moment or two, they will shrink. The timing of the baking will depend on the availability of an oven. This activity could lead to a discussion of measurement and scale; items could be measured or traced before and after they are shrunk. If the logistics of baking the Shrinky Dinks becomes too challenging, an alternative activity could be playing with sponge toys that are made to expand when placed in water.

Trace dinosaur shadows. Holding toy dinosaurs up to a light source, such as a projector, creates a shadow on the wall. Students can make the shadows bigger or smaller, depending on how close they hold the toy to the light source. Dinosaurs grow and shrink as a tangible representation of Daisy responding to the *grow* and *shrink* block commands in the app. Students might enjoy tracing the dinosaur shadows onto paper secured to the wall. To do this, the toy must be held still by a classmate, or placed on a surface, such as a table or shelf.

Daisy dance party. Students can make up dance steps based on the commands in the Daisy app, such as *jump* and *spin*. Students will need room to move and fun music to dance to. The dances could be free and spontaneous, or choreographed. One way to document the choreographed dances would be to print out labels with the Daisy commands and have students place the labels in a sequence to represent their dance (see Figure 3).

Make and shake butter. The process of making butter is a tangible, kinesthetic experience that demonstrates the concept of *conditions* that appears frequently in computer coding. Conditions are often expressed as *if/then* relationships. The condition here is: *If* you shake the jar of cream, *then* it will turn into butter. The process of shaking the jars mirrors shaking the tablet for the *when* command in the Daisy app. Each student will be given a small jar of cream to shake. After a great deal of shaking, the cream will begin to curdle into butter.

Alternate "shake" activity. If the butter-making activity is not possible, due to class logistics or students' interests, a set of Etch A Sketch toys could be used as an alternate activity. This classic toy presents several interesting parallels to the Daisy app: The toy can be shaken to create a cause-and-effect situation that is similar to the *when* command in the Daisy app. Also, the navigation of the "cursor" on the Etch A Sketch screen requires some troubleshooting and spatial navigation skills that are similar to programming Daisy.

DAISY DANCE PARTY!

Make up your own dance. Place the commands in order to show us how to do your dance.

Labels to cut and paste:

move	move	jump	jump
turn	turn	roll	roll
grow	grow	spin	spin
shrink	shrink		

Figure 3. Sample Daisy dance party labels.

Make a Kodable fuzz creature (and make a Kodable path). Students will make a fuzzy creature to play with as a tangible representation of the little creature in the Kodable app. Like the dinosaur avatars, the Kodable fuzz creatures are symbols that represent figures on the screen. The creatures can be constructed a number of different ways using materials such as clay, pom poms, cotton balls, and googly eyes. Students can also make Kodable paths for their creatures on large pieces of graph paper by coloring squares in patterns similar to the Kodable apps. Students may want to look at screenshots from the Kodable game to get ideas for their paths.

TEACHER PREPARATION

Teaching Daisy/Teaching Coding

The command blocks in Daisy the Dinosaur are labeled with text such as "move" or "jump" rather than icons or arrows. This presents an initial challenge for young students who are not yet readers. Yet, surprisingly, our experience using this app with prereaders has been very positive. Students learn what the blocks can do through a variety of methods, through trial and error as well as by using or developing whatever sight letters or sight words they are able to learn at this point. Instructors are encouraged to create and post a key to the text blocks, where each word is represented by a corresponding symbol or icon.

Suggested sequence of instruction:

1. **Use "Challenge Mode" to introduce concepts.** In the Daisy the Dinosaur app, the Challenge Mode takes the user through a step-by-step sequence to learn to use each command. The instructions appear as text, and most Pre-K–K students will probably not be able to work through the Challenge Mode independently. Each Challenge Mode step or task can be introduced to students using a projector or SmartBoard. The first time students use Daisy, they may also need instruction in how to use the menu and the play buttons.

2. **Teach *move* and *jump* commands.** These are the first two commands. They allow the user to move Daisy horizontally and vertically.

3. **Teach *repeat* command and the concept of loop.** The *repeat* command in Daisy introduces the concept of loop or looping in computer programming. Use the word *loop* and explain that in coding, looping is used to make a computer do the same thing over and over again. A human being might get tired or bored from looping, but computers can loop forever without tiring.

4. **Introduce troubleshooting.** Learning to solve problems and fix mistakes, or *troubleshooting*, is a very important part of computer programming. Celebrate mistakes as opportunities to learn more about how the app works and how to write code. Demonstrate making mistakes, and ask students to help you figure out what went wrong. Make a list of all of the great ways students solve problems when things don't go as expected.

5. **Teach *grow* and *shrink* commands.** The *grow* and *shrink* commands may be especially interesting to students because they demonstrate concepts of measurement and scale, and the two commands function in relation to each other. It is also possible to grow Daisy until she becomes so large she can no longer be seen on the screen. Ask students questions

to spark complex and critical thinking: How much does Daisy grow each time we use the *grow* command? How could we measure that? How much does she shrink? If we make her grow three times and shrink two times, will she be bigger or smaller than when she started?

6. **Teach when (conditions).** The concept of *conditions* is very important in computer coding. Conditions are often expressed as *if/then* relationships. In the Daisy app, the concept of conditions is introduced using a simple *when* command that has only two options for conditions—shake or touch. One common mistake students make at this point is that they forget to touch the "play" button before they start shaking or touching. This common mistake is another opportunity for troubleshooting. Don't tell students what they've done wrong; let them try to figure it out. Although *shake* is listed first, encourage students to also use the *touch* condition; this is more similar to the conditions usually found on a tablet app with a touchscreen. Also, make sure students are gentle and careful when they shake the tablets.

IDEAS FOR DIFFERENTIATION

The structure of the lessons, with opportunities to explore a variety of learning centers, is designed to allow students to learn and explore at their own pace. Students who need more time to master new ideas can be allowed to spend a longer amount of time in a learning center, or be allowed to make their own choice for which center to visit, as long as that strategy does not disrupt the rest of the classroom.

For students needing greater challenge, here are some suggestions:

> **More challenging apps and games:** Students who are already familiar with Daisy or who are able to move through the Challenge Mode lessons very quickly may need more challenging apps to use. Kodable is a good next step after Daisy, and many students may enjoy using this app. There are also some great games for young students available at Code.org (see Resources section).

> **Challenge students to "break" the app:** Students who say or show that the Daisy app is too easy or simple can be encouraged to "break" the app. "Breaking" the app means testing and documenting its limits in a systematic way. How many commands can the user fit into one program? What happens when Daisy grows too large to fit on the screen? Have students make a list of the limitations and brainstorm ideas for changes and additions they would make if they were programmers. Have them write

or dictate a letter to the Daisy developers (at Hopscotch Technologies, hello@gethopscotch.com) and share their feedback.

> **Add challenge to literacy activities:** Students who are ready for a greater storytelling or story writing challenge can be encouraged to develop more complex and elaborate stories on paper or using electronic resources, such as the Toontastic 3D app. An extra, optional learning center could be created for students who want more time to write and draw their own stories. Share these stories during the closing circle at the end of each class. If possible, briefly act out the stories that students have written or dictated (no props or scenery, just simple gestures).

UNIT II
Story Code Beta

COURSE DESCRIPTION

ScratchJr is the newest version of the educational Scratch programming language developed by the MIT Media Lab. Young programmers will use ScratchJr, as well as traditional methods like drawing, writing, and dramatization, to bring their stories to life.

Essential Questions

> What do computer programmers do?
> How is writing computer code similar to writing a story? How is it different?
> What do games and stories teach us about computers and coding?

Learning Outcomes

During the course, students will:
> learn and discuss how computer programmers write code to make computers do certain things;
> define and use computer programming terms and concepts, such as *coding*, *sequence*, *loop*, and *troubleshooting*;
> practice writing code using ScratchJr; and
> create stories through writing, drawing, and coding.

Materials

> Teacher's copies of read-aloud books (see Welcome Circle)
> 4–6 iPads with ScratchJr app
> Student copies of Coding Preassessment and Coding Postassessment (see pp. 154–155)

> Paper, pencils, and other writing materials
> Stencils and/or rubber stamps
> Wooden blocks, cube blocks, and/or Straws and Connectors
> Robot Turtles
> Blokus and/or Qwirkle
> Puppets, masks, and dramatic play props

LESSON PLANS AT A GLANCE

Monday	Tuesday	Wednesday	Thursday	Friday
Welcome Circle: Introductions and read *Caps for Sale*.	**Welcome Circle:** Read *Harold and the Purple Crayon*.	**Welcome Circle:** Read *Five Little Monkeys Jumping on the Bed*.	**Welcome Circle:** Read *Good Night, Gorilla*.	**Welcome Circle:** Create a class story to share at Expo.
Mini-Lesson: Introduce ScratchJr (motion blocks, how to save a project).	**Mini-Lesson:** ScratchJr, cont. (choosing a background, create new background).	**Mini-Lesson:** Troubleshooting (share strategies for solving problems).	**Mini-Lesson:** ScratchJr, cont. (add text and dialogue).	**Centers:** 1. Tablets: Animate class story 2. Dramatize class story 3. Games 4. Postassessment
Centers: 1. Tablets 2. Preassessment 3. Drawing and writing 4. Blocks	**Centers:** 1. Tablets 2. Games 3. Drama: Puppets/ masks 4. Write/draw a story	**Centers:** 1. Tablets 2. Games 3. Blocks 4. Write/draw a story	**Centers:** 1. Tablets 2. Blocks 3. Drama: Puppets/ masks 4. Write/draw a story	**Recess/Break**
Recess/Break	**Recess/Break**	**Recess/Break**	**Recess/Break**	**Prepare for Expo**
Mini-Lesson: ScratchJr, cont. (start and end blocks, choosing a character).	**Mini-Lesson:** ScratchJr, cont. (repeat blocks).	**Mini-Lesson:** ScratchJr, cont. (adding sounds).	**Mini-Lesson:** ScratchJr, cont. (speed, change page).	**Expo:** Present class story; display student work in centers; students teach parents how to use apps.
Revisit Centers	**Revisit Centers**	**Revisit Centers**	**Revisit Centers**	
Closing Circle: Read, act out, or demonstrate today's stories.	**Closing Circle:** Read, act out, or demonstrate today's stories.	**Closing Circle:** Read, act out, or demonstrate today's stories.	**Closing Circle:** Read, act out, or demonstrate today's stories.	

LESSON DETAILS

Welcome Circle and Closing Circle

Starting each class session with a welcome circle provides an opportunity to establish a sense of community, review the schedule and expectations, and take attendance. Students sit on the floor while the instructor leads the discussion. The instructor concludes the welcome circle with a read aloud of a storybook. The closing circle at the end of the day can be used to share stories that have been drawn, written, or coded during the course of the day. Suggested books include:

> ***Caps for Sale: A Tale of a Peddler, Some Monkeys and Their Monkey Business* by Esphyr Slobodkina:** This is an engaging story (a great example of good writing for aspiring authors) that demonstrates some of the concepts students will use in coding: *sequencing, looping, troubleshooting,* and *tenacity*. Discuss: How does the peddler "program" the monkeys?

> ***Harold and the Purple Crayon* by Crockett Johnson:** Harold's creation of his world has some similarities to the way students can draw and create their backgrounds in ScratchJr. Discuss: If Harold used ScratchJr, what would he draw?

> ***Five Little Monkeys Jumping on the Bed* by Eileen Christelow:** This book also has a monkey theme, extending a theme from *Caps for Sale*. Discuss: Could you animate this story in ScratchJr? Why or why not?

> ***Good Night, Gorilla* by Peggy Rathmann:** Discuss: If you were going to add dialogue to this story, what would you add?

Mini-Lessons

See "Teaching ScratchJr" in the Teacher Preparation section (p. 59) for information about the curriculum and how to introduce specific concepts. Large-group instruction should be brief, an opportunity to introduce students to the concepts they will be practicing in centers using individual tablets.

Centers

Tablets. Students' screen time will be primarily limited to small-group work in centers of four to six students. This is the time to learn and practice the specific coding concepts that the instructor has introduced in a mini-lesson. The instructor or another adult should closely supervise this center. Students will likely need assistance, especially in the first part of the week when they are new to ScratchJr. The other centers have been planned to reduce the need for direct supervision in order to allow the instructor to focus on students with tablets.

Pre- and postassessment. The pre- and postassessments are intended to measure and document students' general understanding of what we can do with tablets and computers. Both assessments are handouts (see pp. 154–155) that ask students to draw a picture and explain it. If students are not independent writers, they may dictate responses to an adult. In practice, it may be difficult to find classroom time for every student to dictate a response. Instructors should try to collect as many responses as is reasonable in the time available. Another option might be to ask parents to write down students' postassessment responses at home or during Expo.

Drawing and writing. This center should always be well stocked with paper, pencils, and markers. Supplemental materials such as stencils and rubber stamps can be added at various times during the week to add variety and novelty. If a teaching assistant is available, this would be a good position for him or her to take, in case students would like to dictate a story. Students should be encouraged to use their time at this center to create stories. Students can be encouraged to retell or illustrate the storybooks the class read together, or to write down the stories they have seen or created in ScratchJr.

Blocks. The center should be stocked with a rotating variety of wooden blocks, colored cubes, Straws and Connectors, and other manipulatives that allow students to create structures, patterns, and shapes. Small animal and people figures could also be included for variety. Students can be encouraged to build and pretend in any way they choose. This is an opportunity for students to develop and try out their own ideas for imaginary scenarios. The instructors' conversations with students and their facilitation of play should help students make connections between the virtual worlds they are creating on the screen and the real, tangible worlds they are creating in the blocks center. For example, if students use Toca Builders to build a virtual landscape, they can also be invited to re-create the same landscape in the blocks center using wooden blocks or cubes.

Games. Robot Turtles is a board game that introduces basic coding concepts. The game instructions describe different levels of challenge, such as the Basic Game, adding the Unlockables, adding the Write Program, and adding the Function Frog. Playing the game requires someone, an adult or experienced child, to serve as the Turtle Mover. If an adult is not available to facilitate the game at the games center, other games that teach patterns and spatial reasoning, such as Blokus or Qwirkle, could be offered at this learning center.

Drama. The drama center is a place where students have an opportunity to create and act out stories. The materials available can be rotated so different items are available each day. Materials offered could include puppets, masks, and dramatic play props (hats, capes, magic wands). At other times, puppet-making or mask-making craft supplies might be offered. Another option for the drama center is to offer Model Magic clay. Students may create whatever they please, but they can be encouraged to create figures that represent the stories they are writing and programming in class.

TEACHER PREPARATION

Teaching ScratchJr

When these courses were piloted, we used the ScratchJr K–2 curriculum to teach ScratchJr lessons ("Animated Genres," available at https://www.scratchjr.org/teach/curricula/animated-genres). We now have available a new publication, *The Official ScratchJr Book* by Marina Umaschi Bers and Mitchel Resnick. This book is very clearly written and well organized. Instructors may prefer using this book instead of the "Animated Genres" curriculum. The scope and sequence is very similar in both resources, but the new book is a bit more user-friendly.

The anticipated pace for this Story Code Beta course is that students will progress through the first two modules of the "Animated Genres" curriculum or through the first two chapters of *The Official ScratchJr Book*. Some may advance even further on their own, especially if they already have some experience with ScratchJr. Students should be allowed to experiment and work independently.

IDEAS FOR DIFFERENTIATION

The structure of the lessons, with opportunities to explore a variety of learning centers, is designed to allow students to learn and explore at their own pace. Students who need more time to master new ideas can be allowed to spend a longer amount of time in a learning center, or be allowed to make their own choice for which center to visit, as long as that strategy does not disrupt the rest of the classroom.

For students needing greater challenge, here are some suggestions:

> **Teaching coding concepts using other apps:** ScratchJr allows young students to explore a surprisingly broad variety of techniques, ideas, and projects. A student is not likely to run out of ideas for ScratchJr during one week of class, even if the student has had previous experience with the app. However, if a student loses interest in ScratchJr, there are some other art, construction, or animation apps that would provide similar challenges and opportunities for creativity. Toca Builders, for example, is an app similar to Minecraft but tailored for a younger audience, which allows students to build a virtual world out of cube blocks. The apps Mini Doodlecast and ArtMaker allow students to draw and animate pictures and stories using some tools and techniques that are different from ScratchJr. Students who are overwhelmed by the many different choices and tools available in ScratchJr, or who, for whatever reason, seem inter-

ested in trying a different kind of coding experience, may enjoy playing educational coding games such as Kodable, Run Marco!, or The Foos.

> **Add challenge to literacy activities:** Students who are ready for a greater storytelling or story writing challenge can be encouraged to develop more complex and elaborate stories on paper or using electronic resources, such as the Toontastic 3D app. An extra, optional learning center could be created for students who want more time to write and draw their own stories. Share these stories during the closing circle at the end of each class. If possible, briefly act out the stories that students have written or dictated (no props or scenery, just simple gestures).

UNIT III
Story Code Gamma

COURSE DESCRIPTION

How is a story on paper different from a story on a computer screen? Students use creativity and critical thinking to develop and present stories using apps, such as ScratchJr and Hopscotch.

Essential Questions

> What is computer code?
> What are the benefits of using a computer to create a story?
> What do we learn about computers and coding when we make mistakes?

Learning Outcomes

During the course, students will:
> define *code* in the context of computer programming;
> describe and demonstrate how to create a sequence of block code in ScratchJr;
> define and use the term *troubleshooting*;
> create and use strategies for solving programming problems;
> learn and demonstrate coding concepts such as *sequence*, *loop*, and *conditions*;
> create animated projects by writing block code in ScratchJr and/or other apps like Hopscotch; and
> create stories through writing, drawing, and coding.

Materials

> Teacher's copies of read-aloud books (see Welcome Circle)
> 4–6 iPads with ScratchJr and Hopscotch apps

> Student copies of Coding Preassessment and Coding Postassessment (see pp. 154–155)
> Paper, pencils, and other writing materials
> Robot jigsaw puzzle
> Stencils and/or rubber stamps
> Robot Turtles
> Blokus and/or Qwirkle
> Wooden blocks, cube blocks, and/or Straws and Connectors

LESSON PLANS AT A GLANCE

Monday	Tuesday	Wednesday	Thursday	Friday
Welcome Circle: Introductions and read *Sheep in a Jeep*.	**Welcome Circle:** Read *King Bidgood's in the Bathtub*.	**Welcome Circle:** Read *The Most Magnificent Thing*.	**Welcome Circle:** Read *If You Give a Mouse a Cookie* (demonstrating *if/then* conditions).	**Welcome Circle:** Create a class story to share at Expo.
Mini-Lesson: Introduce ScratchJr (motion blocks, how to save, backgrounds).	**Mini-Lesson:** ScratchJr, cont. (start and end blocks, choosing a character, repeat blocks).	**Mini-Lesson:** Introducing Hopscotch (Monster Hugs, menu walk-through, loops).	**Mini-Lesson:** ScratchJr, cont. (start on bump, start on tap).	**Centers:** 1. Tablets: Animate class story 2. Problem-solving lab 3. Illustrate class story 4. Postassessment
Centers: 1. Tablets 2. Preassessment 3. Problem-solving lab 4. Puzzles	**Centers:** 1. Tablets 2. Games 3. Blocks and manipulatives 4. Writing and drawing	**Centers:** 1. Tablets 2. Games 3. Blocks and manipulatives 4. Writing and drawing	**Centers:** 1. Tablets 2. Games 3. Blocks and manipulatives 4. Writing and drawing	**Recess/Break**
Recess/Break	**Recess/Break**	**Recess/Break**	**Recess/Break**	**Prepare for Expo**
Mini-Lesson: Troubleshooting (strategies for solving problems).	**Mini-Lesson:** ScratchJr, cont. (add text and dialogue, adding sounds).	**Mini-Lesson:** ScratchJr, cont. (speed, change page).	**Mini-Lesson:** ScratchJr, cont. (send and receive messages).	**Expo:** Present/ display class story; display student work in centers; students teach parents how to use apps.
Centers: 1. Tablets 2. Games 3. Blocks and manipulatives 4. Writing and drawing	**Revisit Centers**	**Revisit Centers**	**Revisit Centers**	
Closing Circle: Read, act out, or demonstrate today's stories.	**Closing Circle:** Read, act out, or demonstrate today's stories.	**Closing Circle:** Read, act out, or demonstrate today's stories.	**Closing Circle:** Read, act out, or demonstrate today's stories.	

LESSON DETAILS

Welcome Circle and Closing Circle

Starting each class session with a welcome circle provides an opportunity to establish a sense of community, review the schedule and expectations, and take attendance. Students sit on the floor while the instructor leads the discussion. The instructor concludes the welcome circle with a read aloud of a storybook. Suggested books include:

> ***Sheep in a Jeep** by Nancy Shaw:* This engaging and humorous story demonstrates the concept of *troubleshooting* as the sheep encounter and work to solve various jeep-related problems.

> ***King Bidgood's in the Bathtub** by Audrey Wood:* In this story, members of the king's court try different ways to convince King Bidgood to leave the comforts of his bath.

> ***The Most Magnificent Thing** by Ashley Spires:* The main character in this story follows a design engineering process that incorporates many different iterations.

> ***If You Give a Mouse a Cookie** by Laura Numeroff:* This familiar classic demonstrates the concept of *conditions* (if/then), which is directly related to the ScratchJr programming lesson for the day (start on the bump, start on the tap).

Mini-Lessons

See "Teaching ScratchJr and Hopscotch" in the Teacher Preparation section (p. 66) for information about the apps and how to introduce specific concepts. Large-group instruction should be brief, an opportunity to introduce students to the concepts they will be practicing in centers using individual tablets.

Centers

Tablets. Students' screen time will be primarily limited to small-group work in centers of four to six students. This is the time to learn and practice the specific coding concepts that the instructor has introduced in a mini-lesson. The instructor or another adult should closely supervise this center. Students will likely need assistance, especially in the first part of the week when they are new to ScratchJr. The other centers have been planned to reduce the need for direct supervision in order to allow the instructor to focus on students with tablets.

Pre- and postassessments. The pre- and postassessments are intended to measure and document students' general understanding of what we can do with tablets and computers. Both assessments are handouts (see pp. 154–155) that ask students to draw a picture and explain it. If students are not independent writers, they may dictate responses to an adult. In practice, it may be difficult to find classroom time for every student to dictate a response. Instructors should try to collect as many responses as is reasonable in the time available. Another option might be to ask parents to write down students' postassessment responses at home or during Expo.

Problem-solving lab. The problem-solving lab is used on the first and last day of class to challenge students to articulate and develop troubleshooting and debugging strategies that they can use to solve all different kinds of problems, in both computer programming and in the real, tangible world. Present students with a very tangled knot of yarn and string and ask them to collaboratively come up with a plan for detangling it. Students can be invited to use a "troubleshooting tool" to organize and document their problem-solving process (see Figure 4). At the end of the week, the problem-solving lab activity is to put together a small tent without using the instructions.

Puzzles. The puzzle center is similar to the problem-solving lab. Students are presented with a puzzle to solve together. Again, they can be invited to use the "troubleshooting tool" to organize and document their problem-solving process. A jigsaw puzzle featuring a robot image is ideal, but any challenging jigsaw puzzle could be used as a problem-solving activity. To increase the level of challenge, remove several puzzle pieces and ask students to create replacement puzzle pieces on paper or cardboard.

Drawing and writing. This center should always be well stocked with paper, pencils, and markers. Supplemental materials, such as stencils, stickers, and rubber stamps, can be added at various times during the week to add variety and novelty. Students should be encouraged to use their time at this center to create stories. Students can be encouraged to retell or illustrate the storybooks the class read together, or to write down the stories they have seen or created in ScratchJr or Hopscotch.

Games. Robot Turtles is a board game that introduces basic coding concepts. The game instructions describe different levels of challenge, such as the Basic Game, adding the Unlockables, adding the Write Program, and adding the Function Frog. Playing the game requires someone, an adult or experienced child, to serve as the Turtle Mover. If an adult is not available to facilitate the game at the games center, other games that teach patterns and spatial reasoning, such as Blokus or Qwirkle, could be offered at this learning center.

Blocks and manipulatives. The center should be stocked with a rotating variety of wooden blocks, colored cubes, Straws and Connectors, and other

Name: _____   Date: _____

TROUBLESHOOTING TOOL

Directions: Take a minute to look at the problem in front of you.

Write one sentence that describes the problem:

_____

_____

_____

Think of five strategies you could use to try to solve this problem.

    1.

    2.

    3.

    4.

    5.

Circle the one you want to try first. Then try it.

Did it work?   ❑ Yes   ❑ No

If not, what do you want to try next?

_____

_____

_____

Keep trying different strategies until you solve the problem or you run out of time.

Figure 4. Sample troubleshooting tool.

manipulatives that allow students to create structures, patterns, and shapes. Small animal and people figures could also be included for variety. Students can be encouraged to build and pretend in any way they choose. This is an opportunity for students to develop and try out their own ideas for imaginary scenarios. The instructors' conversations with students and their facilitation of play should help students make connections between the virtual worlds they are creating on the screen and the real, tangible worlds they are creating in the blocks center. For example, if students use Toca Builders to build a virtual landscape, they can also be invited to recreate the same landscape in the blocks center using wooden blocks, cube blocks, or Unifix Cubes.

TEACHER PREPARATION

Teaching ScratchJr and Hopscotch

When these courses were piloted, we used the ScratchJr K–2 curriculum to teach ScratchJr lessons ("Animated Genres," available at https://www.scratchjr.org/teach/curricula/animated-genres). We now have available a new publication, *The Official ScratchJr Book* by Marina Umaschi Bers and Mitchel Resnick. This book is very clearly written and well organized. Instructors may prefer using this book instead of the "Animated Genres" curriculum. The scope and sequence is very similar in both resources, but the new book is a bit more user-friendly.

The anticipated pace for this Story Code Gamma course is that students will progress through the first two modules of the "Animated Genres" curriculum or, if you are using *The Official ScratchJr Book*, through the first two chapters. Some may advance even further on their own, especially if they already have some experience with ScratchJr. Students should be allowed to experiment and work independently.

IDEAS FOR DIFFERENTIATION

The structure of the lessons, with opportunities to explore a variety of learning centers, is designed to allow students to learn and explore at their own pace. Students who need more time to master new ideas can be allowed to spend a longer amount of time in a learning center, or be allowed to make their own choice for which center to visit, as long as that strategy does not disrupt the rest of the classroom.

For students needing greater challenge, here are some suggestions:

> **Teaching coding concepts using other apps:** ScratchJr allows young students to explore a surprisingly broad variety of techniques, ideas, and projects. A student is not likely to run out of ideas for ScratchJr during one week of class, even if the student has had previous experience with the app. However, if a student loses interest in ScratchJr, he or she can be encouraged to use Hopscotch instead. Also, there are some other art, construction, or animation apps that would provide similar challenges and opportunities for creativity. For example, Cargo-Bot is a game that teaches coding concepts. Toca Builders is an app, similar to Minecraft but tailored for a younger audience, which allows students to build a virtual world out of cube blocks. The apps Mini Doodlecast, ArtMaker, and Superhero Comic Book Maker allow students to draw and animate pictures and stories using some tools and techniques that are different from ScratchJr. Students who are overwhelmed by the many different choices and tools available in ScratchJr, or who, for whatever reason, seem interested in trying a different kind of coding experience, may enjoy playing educational coding games, such as Kodable, Run Marco!, or Cargo-Bot.

> **Add challenge to literacy activities:** Students who are ready for a greater storytelling or story writing challenge can be encouraged to develop more complex and elaborate stories on paper or using electronic resources, such as the Superhero Comic Book Maker app from Duck Duck Moose. Students who are capable or advanced writers should be encouraged to add details and dialogue to both their written work and their digital creations.

UNIT IV
Story Code Delta

COURSE DESCRIPTION

Students create detailed narratives with multiple characters and settings. They learn to animate their stories using ScratchJr and/or the original Scratch programming language. Although this course is designed for children in second grade, these lesson plans also include options for differentiation that allow for scaffolding for third graders.

Essential Questions

> What do people need to learn in order to program a computer?
> How are animated stories similar to stories in a book? How are they different?
> Do computers make our lives better? Why or why not?

Learning Outcomes

During the course, students will:
> learn how to create a sequence of block code in ScratchJr and/or Scratch;
> demonstrate coding concepts such as *sequence*, *loop*, *conditions*, and *troubleshooting*;
> create stories with multiple characters and settings through writing, drawing, and coding; and
> evaluate the benefits and challenges of using animation to tell stories, as compared to writing stories on paper.

Materials

> Teacher's copies of read-aloud books (see Welcome Circle)
> 4–6 iPads with ScratchJr and Hopscotch apps

> Student copies of Coding Preassessment and Coding Postassessment (see pp. 154–155)
> Computer and Internet access for at least 4–6 students to use web-based Scratch (available at https://scratch.mit.edu)
> Small blocks, tiles, colored cubes, and other manipulatives
> Paper, pencils, and other writing materials
> Stencils and/or rubber stamps
> Robot Turtles
> Blokus and/or Qwirkle (optional)

LESSON PLANS AT A GLANCE

Monday	Tuesday	Wednesday	Thursday	Friday
Welcome Circle: Introductions and read *Where the Wild Things Are*.	**Welcome Circle:** Read *Leonardo, the Terrible Monster*.	**Welcome Circle:** Read *Shark vs. Train*.	**Welcome Circle:** Read *Go Away, Big Green Monster!*	**Welcome Circle:** Create a class story to share at Expo.
Mini-Lesson: Introduce ScratchJr (Module 1).	**Mini-Lesson:** ScratchJr, cont. (Module 2).	**Mini-Lesson:** Introducing Hopscotch (Monster Hugs, menu walkthrough)	**Mini-Lesson:** Introduce web-based Scratch (Getting Started).	**Centers:** 1. Tablets: Animate class story 2. Dramatize class story 3. Illustrate class story 4. Postassessment 5. Laptops and web-based tools (if available)
Centers: 1. Tablets 2. Preassessment 3. Manipulatives and monsters 4. Writing and drawing 5. Laptops and web-based tools (if available)	**Centers:** 1. Tablets 2. Games 3. Manipulatives and monsters 4. Writing and drawing 5. Laptops and web-based tools (if available)	**Centers:** 1. Tablets 2. Games 3. Manipulatives and monsters 4. Writing and drawing 5. Laptops and web-based tools (if available)	**Centers:** 1. Tablets 2. Games 3. Manipulatives and monsters 4. Writing and drawing 5. Laptops and web-based tools (if available)	**Recess/Break**
Recess/Break	**Recess/Break**	**Recess/Break**	**Recess/Break**	**Prepare for Expo**
Mini-Lesson: Troubleshooting (strategies for solving problems).	**Mini-Lesson:** ScratchJr, cont. (Module 3).	**Mini-Lesson:** Hopscotch, cont. (loops, randomness, Etch A Sketch)	**Mini-Lesson:** Comparing the three platforms: How are they the same? How are they different?	**Expo:** Present/display class story; display student work in centers; students teach parents how to use apps.
Revisit Centers: Substitute games for preassessment.	**Revisit Centers**	**Revisit Centers**	**Revisit Centers**	
Closing Circle: Read, act out, or demonstrate today's stories.	**Closing Circle:** Read, act out, or demonstrate today's stories.	**Closing Circle:** Read, act out, or demonstrate today's stories.	**Closing Circle:** Read, act out, or demonstrate today's stories.	

LESSON DETAILS

Welcome Circle and Closing Circle

Starting each class session with a welcome circle provides an opportunity to establish a sense of community, review the schedule and expectations, and take attendance. Students sit on the floor while the instructor leads the discussion. The instructor concludes the welcome circle with a read aloud of a storybook. The suggested books for this course all share a monster theme. The books present monsters who are fanciful, strange, and often humorous creatures. Students may be inspired by the books to create their own fanciful and strange creatures in their own written, illustrated, and animated stories. Suggested books include:

> *Where the Wild Things Are* **by Maurice Sendak:** In this familiar classic picture book, the monsters demonstrate actions that can be created in ScratchJr using block code, such as jumping up and down.

> *Leonardo, the Terrible Monster* **by Mo Willems:** The monster in this story resembles the animated monsters in the Hopscotch app. The book also demonstrates that a story needs an ending or resolution.

> *Go Away, Big Green Monster!* **by Ed Emberley:** The design of this book, with cutaway pages that layer the images, provides a tangible demonstration of many of the animation features in ScratchJr.

> *Shark vs. Train* **by Chris Barton:** This picture book inspires critical thinking and discussion around how authors express humor and represent conflict.

Mini-Lessons

See "Teaching ScratchJr, Hopscotch, and Scratch" in the Teacher Preparation section (p. 73) for information about the curriculum and how to introduce specific concepts. Large-group instruction should be brief, an opportunity to introduce students to the concepts they will be practicing in centers using individual tablets or computers.

Centers

Tablets (and computers and web-based tools). Students' screen time will be primarily limited to small-group work in centers. This is the time to learn and practice the specific coding concepts that the instructor has introduced on the SmartBoard. The instructor or another adult should closely supervise this center. Students will likely need assistance, especially in the first part of the week when they are new to the apps and programs. The other centers have been planned to reduce the need for direct supervision in order to allow the instructor to focus on students with tablets and desktop computers or laptops.

Pre- and postassessments. The pre- and postassessments are intended to measure and document students' general understanding of what we can do with tablets and computers. Both assessments are handouts (see pp. 154–155) that ask students to draw a picture and explain it. If students are not independent writers, they may dictate responses to an adult. In practice, it may be difficult to find classroom time for every student to dictate a response. Instructors should try to collect as many responses as is reasonable in the time available. Another option might be to ask parents to write down students' postassessment responses at home or during Expo.

Manipulatives and monsters. The center should be stocked with a rotating variety of small blocks, tiles, colored cubes, and other manipulatives that allow students to create structures, patterns, and shapes. Small monster and people figures can also be included to encourage the development of narratives that connect the spatial and geometric concepts of the manipulatives to the stories that are being animated in the apps and programs. Students can be encouraged to build, play, and pretend in any way they choose. The instructors' conversations and facilitation of play should help students make connections between the virtual worlds they are creating on the screen and the real, tangible worlds they are creating in the center. For example, if students use Toca Builders to build a virtual landscape, they can also be invited to recreate the same landscape in the blocks center using Unifix Cubes.

Writing and drawing. This center should always be well stocked with paper, pencils, and markers. Supplemental materials, such as stencils, stickers, and rubber stamps, can be added at various times during the week to add variety and novelty. Students should be encouraged to use their time at this center to create stories. Students can be encouraged to retell or illustrate the storybooks the class read together, to begin sketching out their ideas for what they want to animate next, or to write down the stories they have seen or created in ScratchJr, Hopscotch, or Scratch.

Games. Robot Turtles is a board game that introduces basic coding concepts. The game instructions describe different levels of challenge, such as the Basic Game, adding the Unlockables, adding the Write Program, and adding the Function Frog. Playing the game requires someone, an adult or experienced child, to serve as the Turtle Mover. If an adult is not available to facilitate the game at the games center, other games that teach patterns and spatial reasoning, such as Blokus or Qwirkle, could be offered at this learning center.

TEACHER PREPARATION

Teaching ScratchJr, Hopscotch, and Scratch

ScratchJr and Hopscotch (both tablet apps), as well as web-based Scratch, are excellent tools for students to use to create their own animated projects using block programming. ScratchJr is the most accessible, requiring very little reading and computer experience from students in order to get started with fun projects right away. ScratchJr also allows for a great deal of variety and complexity for students to continue to learn and experiment as they create more complex backgrounds and multiple characters, add effects such as sound and dialogue, and program conditions that allow for the story to take multiple paths.

It would be possible to spend the entire week of class just using ScratchJr, but if students are in need of more variety or challenge than ScratchJr can offer, Hopscotch and web-based Scratch can also be introduced.

Use the ScratchJr K–2 curriculum ("Animated Genres," available at https://www.scratchjr.org/teach/curricula/animated-genres) or *The Official ScratchJr Book* to teach ScratchJr lessons, and "Hopscotch Curriculum" (available at https://www.gethopscotch.com/resources) to introduce Hopscotch. Web-based Scratch can be taught using the "Getting Started With Scratch" tutorials (available at https://wiki.scratch.mit.edu/wiki/Getting_Started_with_Scratch).

When these courses were piloted, we used "Animated Genres" to teach ScratchJr lessons. We now have available a newer publication, *The Official ScratchJr Book* by Marina Umaschi Bers and Mitchel Resnick. This book is very clearly written and well organized. Instructors may prefer using this book instead of the "Animated Genres" curriculum. The scope and sequence is very similar in both resources, but the new book is a bit more user-friendly. If laptops or notebook computers are available, an additional learning center could be created for web-based Scratch and/or Code.org tutorials.

The anticipated pace for this Story Code Delta course is that students will progress through most of the modules/chapters in the ScratchJr curriculum during the first 2 or 3 days of class. On the third day, Hopscotch could be introduced. Then, on Thursday and Friday, instructors can either introduce web-based Scratch or continue to teach the variety of tools and effects in ScratchJr and Hopscotch.

Some students may already have had some experience with ScratchJr, Scratch, and/or Hopscotch. Students should be allowed to experiment and work independently at their own pace.

The ScratchJr curriculum resources also include project cards that can be used to challenge students to try new tools and coding experiences.

IDEAS FOR DIFFERENTIATION

The structure of the lessons, with opportunities to explore a variety of learning centers, is designed to allow students to learn and explore at their own pace. Students who need more time to master new ideas can be allowed to spend a longer amount of time in a learning center, or be allowed to make their own choice for which center to visit, as long as that strategy does not disrupt the rest of the classroom.

For students needing greater challenge, here are some suggestions:

> **Teaching coding concepts using other apps:** There are some other art, construction, or animation apps that would provide similar challenges and opportunities for creativity. For example, Cargo-Bot is a game that teaches coding concepts. Toca Builders is an app, similar to Minecraft but tailored for a younger audience, which allows students to build a virtual world out of cube blocks. The apps Mini Doodlecast, ArtMaker, and Superhero Comic Book Maker allow students to draw and animate pictures and stories using some tools and techniques that are different from ScratchJr. Students who are overwhelmed by the many different choices and tools available in ScratchJr, or who, for whatever reason, seem interested in trying a different kind of coding experience, may enjoy playing educational coding games, such Cargo-Bot or the web-based tutorials at Code.org.

> **Add challenge to literacy activities:** Students who are ready for a greater storytelling or story writing challenge can be encouraged to develop more complex and elaborate stories on paper or using electronic resources, such as the Superhero Comic Book Maker app from Duck Duck Moose. Students who are capable or advanced writers should be encouraged to add details and dialogue to both their written work and their digital creations.

TRACK III
Robot Stories

TRACK DESCRIPTION

Robots are everywhere: washing your car at the drive-thru car wash, scanning your suitcase at the airport, and in your house vacuuming your rug. You might not recognize robotic machines because not all robots have faces and voices. Tech Beginnings robotics courses teach students the elements of a robot: machines with a motor and a power source (such as electricity) that can move and perform functions that people program into a computer or an internal computer chip.

The units are:

Bee-Bot Town: Grades Pre-K–K

Students practice and demonstrate introductory coding concepts as they program their Bee-Bot robot friends, create a sequence of commands, and map out roads on a grid.

Primo Pathways: Grades K–1

The Primo Cubetto robot is just one example of "tangible programming," in which students manipulate 3-D objects to create computer code. Primo devices also introduce students to the concept of *function* in coding.

Hexbug Habitats: Grades 1–2

Students analyze the design of various Hexbug creatures, small bio-inspired robots. Engineering features such as sensors are explored and tested.

WeDo Go: Grade 2

Students build and program simple robots using LEGO WeDo robotics kits and engage in critical thinking about the role of robots in our world, now and in the future.

UNIT I
Bee-Bot Town

COURSE DESCRIPTION

Bee-Bots are educational robots designed to introduce young students to computer programming. Students practice and demonstrate introductory coding concepts, such as *symbol*, *sequence*, and *loop*, as they create homes and roads for their Bee-Bot friends.

Essential Questions

> What is a robot?
> How is a Bee-Bot like a real bee? How is it different?
> How do we use code to program a Bee-Bot?

Learning Outcomes

During the course, students will:
> discuss and document the definitions and uses of the term *robot*;
> explore the design, mechanics, and programming of Bee-Bot robots;
> create increasingly complex code to program Bee-Bots to perform specific tasks and actions;
> define and use computer programming terms and concepts, such as *code*, *symbol*, and *sequence*;
> collaborate with classmates to plan, design, and create a town for the Bee-Bot robots;
> use math and spatial reasoning skills to map and measure landmarks in the Bee-Bot town; and
> create stories using words, images, dramatic play, and Bee-Bots.

Materials

> Teacher's copies of read-aloud books (see Welcome Circle)
> Teacher resources (see Bee-Bot Town Resources section)
> Student copies of Robotics Assessment (see p. 156)
> At least 6–8 Bee-Bots and charging station and/or charging cords
> Blocks, cardboard, and/or Straws and Connectors
> Drawing and drafting tools, such as rulers, pencils, paper, etc.
> Model Magic
> Index cards, long strips of paper, string, and/or colored beads

LESSON PLANS AT A GLANCE

Monday	Tuesday	Wednesday	Thursday	Friday
Welcome Circle: Introductions. Watch bee video and/or read "Pollen" by Naomi Shihab Nye.	**Welcome Circle:** Read *My Map Book*.	**Welcome Circle:** Read *Me and My Robot*.	**Welcome Circle:** Read "Waggle Dance" by Douglas Florian.	**Welcome Circle:** Dictate final class story and plan for Expo.
Centers: 1. Preassessment 2. Construction center 3. Model Magic	**Centers:** 1. Bee-Bot challenge: calibration 2. Bee-Bot free play 3. Drawing and drafting 4. Explore programming languages	**Centers:** 1. Bee-Bot challenge: longer code sequences 2. Bee-Bot free play 3. Construction center 4. Explore programming languages	**Centers:** 1. Bee-Bot challenge: synchronization 2. Bee-Bot free play 3. Construction center 4. Explore programming languages	**Centers:** 1. Postassessment 2. Build Bee-Bot town 3. Map the Bee-Bot town
Recess/Break	**Recess/Break**	**Recess/Break**	**Recess/Break**	**Recess/Break**
Mini-Lesson: Meet the Bee-Bots.	**Revisit Centers**	**Revisit Centers**	**Revisit Centers**	**Prepare for Expo**
Centers: 1. Bee-Bot challenge: Point A to point B 2. Bee-Bot free play 3. Drawing and drafting center 4. Construction center	**Closing Circle:** Share one of the programming languages or stories invented today.	**Closing Circle:** Dictate and act out a class Bee-Bot story.	**Closing Circle:** Share one of the programming languages or stories invented today.	**Expo:** Present class story; display Bee-Bot town and maps and code; students teach parents how to use the Bee-Bots.
Closing Circle: Dictate and act out a Bee-Bot story.				

LESSON DETAILS

Welcome Circle and Closing Circle

Starting each class session with a welcome circle provides an opportunity to establish a sense of community, review the schedule and expectations, and take attendance. Students sit on the floor while the instructor leads the discussion. The instructor concludes the welcome circle with a read aloud of a storybook or poem that relates to course content. The comparison of real bees to Bee-Bots creates some interesting higher-order thinking questions that compare the ways bees communicate directions to each other (through movement or "dancing") and the way people program robots. Suggested books and poems include:

> **"Pollen" in *Honeybee: Poems* by Naomi Shihab Nye:** Discuss: How is a bee like "a yellow machine"?
> ***My Map Book* by Sara Fanelli:** Discuss: How could we make a map of a Bee-Bot town?
> ***Me and My Robot* by Tracey West:** Discuss: How do robots know what to do?
> **"Waggle Dance" in *UnBEELievables: Honeybee Poems and Paintings* by Douglas Florian:** Discuss: How are Bee-Bots and real bees the same? How are they different? How can we make our Bee-Bots dance?

Mini-Lesson

See "Teaching Bee-Bots and Programming Languages" in the Teacher Preparation section (p. 81) for information about how to introduce the Bee-Bots and teach specific concepts. Any large-group lessons should be brief. Students will have the opportunity to practice the concepts in learning centers.

Centers

Pre- and postassessment. The pre- and postassessments (see p. 156) are intended to measure and document students' general understanding of robots and computer programming. Students can draw or write their answers. The same handout can be used for both pre- and postassessment. Young students who are not fluent writers can be invited to dictate responses to an adult. In practice, it may be difficult to find classroom time for every student to dictate a response one-on-one with an adult. Instructors can try to collect as many responses as is reasonable in the time available. Another option might be to ask parents to write down students' postassessment responses at home or during Expo.

Construction. This center should be stocked with construction materials, such as blocks, cardboard, and Straws and Connectors. Students can be challenged to build houses, fences, and other features of the Bee-Bot town. Rulers, pencils, and paper can also be used to facilitate and expand student explorations of size and scale as they build. Questions such as "How do you know if this house will be big enough for the Bee-Bots?" can help inspire students to incorporate measurement activities into their construction projects.

Model Magic. Model Magic is a soft clay that can be used by students to create whatever they please. This option allows students to explore ideas in an open-ended way. This center is suggested for Monday on the at-a-glance schedule but could be implemented any time there is a need for a less structured activity.

Bee-Bot challenge and Bee-Bot free play. We recommend that each classroom have access to 6–8 Bee-Bots. This is enough to support two learning centers, each with 3–4 Bee-Bots. Depending on class size and how the rotation through centers is managed, students may need to share and use the Bee-Bots in pairs. The Bee-Bot Challenge learning center should be directly supervised by the instructor, but the Bee-Bot Free Play center is where students have the freedom to use the Bee-Bots however they please and experiment with their own ideas. The at-a-glance schedule suggests a specific concept to address for each Bee-Bot Challenge, such as "point A to point B."

Drawing and drafting. This center should be stocked with a variety of drawing and drafting tools, such as pencils, pens, markers, rulers, stencils, plain paper, lined paper, and graph paper. Students should be encouraged to use their time at the drawing and drafting center to explore making designs and plans for the Bee-Bot town, creating stories about bees or robots, or writing code using symbols, letters, or numerals. Suggested tasks could include drawing a Bee-Bot house or mapping a Bee-Bot road. Instructor suggestions should follow the interests of students as the plans for the Bee-Bot town develop. For example, "Where will we place our traffic lights? Make a drawing that shows your ideas." Or, "Make a map that shows me how far the Bee-Bots need to travel to get to school."

Explore programming languages. At this center students are challenged to come up with multiple ways to represent the code that programs the Bee-Bots. Students will likely easily understand the idea that the arrow buttons on the back of the Bee-Bot control the actions of the Bee-Bot, but they will soon discover that it is hard to remember which buttons they have pushed. They will need a way to document or represent the code they are using to program the Bee-Bot. Explain to students that people communicate with robots through *computer code*. The creation of these codes is called *programming*. Codes can be written or recorded in many different ways. Each is a language. Some of the programming languages students can create and explore at this center include:

> drawing arrows on index cards, each card representing a push of a button on the Bee-Bot's back, and lining up the cards in a row to create a *sequence* or *code*;
> drawing arrows or symbols on a long strip of paper or on a grid;
> creating a sequence of hand signals to represent the commands in the code; and
> stringing colored beads, each color of bead representing a command—green for forward, red for back, purple for right, orange for left.

Challenge students to come up with their own way of representing the code, their own programming language. Perhaps they will discover that sound can also be used as a programming language (a tap means go forward, a stomp means go back).

TEACHER PREPARATION

Teaching Bee-Bots and Programming Languages

Teaching students how to program a Bee-Bot to accomplish increasingly complex tasks will provide a foundation of programming knowledge and skills in the area of computer science. Here is a description of suggested programming tasks, from the most simple to the more complex. You may find that there are other interesting tasks that will engage students in even more exciting learning experiences.

1. **Meet the Bee-Bots: How to use the command buttons.** Initially students will be eager to try out the Bee-Bots without waiting for instructions, which is fine. Once they've had a chance to experiment, there will be natural and spontaneous opportunities to clarify and introduce the functions of each button or command. Briefly demonstrate and explain to students the use of each of the direction buttons, the go button, the pause button, and the reset button. To teach the direction buttons, use consistent language to name each direction—forward, back, right, left. Some young students may not yet have a clear understanding of right and left. You may need to incorporate that concept into the introductory lessons.

2. **Teach the vocabulary for *symbol*, *code*, and *sequence*:** Use simple and direct language to describe and define these concepts. A symbol is something that stands for something else, like a smiley face means happy. An arrow pointing forward is a symbol for moving forward. A code is what

you create when you put symbols in a row, on paper or when you program a Bee-Bot. A sequence is a bunch of symbols or commands in a row, in a particular order, one after another, on a page of paper or in time.

3. **Spatial reasoning:** Navigating on a grid. In order to program a Bee-Bot to move from point A to point B, you have to reason or think about the path the Bee-Bot will take and translate that into a sequence of commands, or code. Students will need to predict, estimate, or measure distances in order to create their codes. One of the challenges most students will find is that a command to turn will only turn; it will not move the Bee-Bot forward. Students will learn through experimentation, trial, and error that turning and moving are two separate commands. One way to add complexity to this process is to put new obstacles in the path of the Bee-Bot and challenge students to program the Bee-Bot to navigate around the obstacles.

4. **Calibration and measurement:** At some point, students will discover that the Bee-Bots are *calibrated*. Every time the forward button is pushed the Bee-Bot moves forward exactly the same distance. Students will be challenged to measure and document what that distance is and incorporate that knowledge into their coding. This should happen almost naturally as students explore what a Bee-Bot can do. Be ready to facilitate that process with materials, such as big pieces of paper, rulers, and yardsticks, that can be used to document and measure the distances the Bee-Bots travel.

5. **Synchronization:** The topic of synchronization will come up if students try to make multiple Bee-Bots race or dance together. Teach students the term *synchronize* to describe how students are aligning the timing of the Bee-Bot programming. This issue may also come up if the class builds a large and complex town in which multiple Bee-Bots are traveling multiple paths at the same time. A Bee-Bot traffic jam is a great opportunity to teach students the concept of synchronization and challenge them to coordinate their programming of the Bee-Bots to avoid traffic jams.

6. **Programming languages:** As described in the explore programming languages center, every time students find a new way to represent their code, they have invented a new programming language. Use the closing circle at the end of each class session to share and demonstrate the different kinds of programming languages students have created and used each day.

IDEAS FOR DIFFERENTIATION

The structure of the lessons, with opportunities to explore a variety of learning centers, is designed to allow students to learn and explore at their own pace. Students who need more time to master new ideas can be allowed to spend a longer amount of time in a learning center, or be allowed to make their own choice for which center to visit, as long as that strategy does not disrupt the rest of the classroom.

For students needing greater challenge, here are some suggestions:

> **Programming languages:** Challenge advanced students to come up with programming languages that are completely different from those used in class. For example, a student who plays a musical instrument could create a piece of music in which specific notes or sounds represent specific commands or codes.

> **Mapping:** Students with advanced spatial reasoning skills could be challenged to create an accurate map of the Bee-Bot paths or towns that the class has created or imagined. They could add advanced map features, such as a compass rose or a key to scale.

> **Documenting with words, images, audio, and video:** A student who is reluctant to participate could be tasked with documenting the class's progress. He or she could write a story, take photos, or make a recording of the Bee-Bots and/or students. Students could also be challenged to write or dictate fiction about the Bee-Bots and what happens in their town.

> **Right angles and measuring angles:** A student with advanced math ability could be challenged to explore and measure the angles involved in Bee-Bot movements and programming. Each turn of the Bee-Bot is a right angle, which is 90 degrees. Introduce the student to the concept of angles and that angles can be measured by degrees. Ask: If a circle is 360 degrees, how many degrees is a right angle? How many degrees does the Bee-Bot travel if it turns right twice? A protractor could be introduced as a tool for measuring angles.

> **Critical thinking:** Challenge advanced students to think about how a Bee-Bot fits into the broader world of robots and computer programming. Ask: Is a Bee-Bot a toy or a robot? Why do you think so?

> **Urban planning:** Ask advanced students to think about what structures and services would be needed in a real town and compare this to the Bee-Bot town students are creating. Ask: What other kinds of structures are needed in a town? Where do the Bee-Bots get their food, water, or electricity?

BEE-BOT TOWN RESOURCES

> Bee-Bot website (available at http://www.bee-bot.us)
> Bee-Bot lesson plans:
>> "Bee-Bot Journeys" (available at https://exchange21.wikispaces.com/file/view/Beebot+Journeys_Lesson+Plan.pdf)
>> "Making Your Classroom Buzz With Bee-Bots: Idea and Activities for the Early Phase" (available at http://codigo21.educacion.navarra.es/wp-content/uploads/2015/09/BeebotguideA4v2.pdf)

> Videos:
>> "Bee-Bot Activity" (available at https://www.youtube.com/watch?v=p4EPfC04URk)
>> "The Waggle Dance of the Honeybee" (available at https://www.youtube.com/watch?v=bFDGPgXtK-U)
>> "Dance of the Honey Bee" (available at https://www.youtube.com/watch?v=Zo6fK1yKcAA)

> Bee picture books and poetry books:
>> *Are You a Bee?* by Judy Allen
>> *The Beautiful Bee Book* by Sue Unstead
>> *Brilliant Bees* by Linda Glaser
>> *Honey in a Hive* by Anne Rockwell
>> *Honeybee: Poems* by Naomi Shihab Nye (*Note*. p. 1 refers to the bees "soaking up directions" and p. 51 compares a bee to a "yellow machine.")
>> *Bees* by Susan Ashley
>> *UnBEElievables: Honeybee Poems and Paintings* by Douglas Florian (*Note*. "Waggle Dance" and its illustration describe how bees communicate directions.)

UNIT II
Primo Pathways

COURSE DESCRIPTION

"Tangible programming" means students use devices and objects they can move, manipulate, and hold to create computer codes. One example is the Primo robot, which students control by placing colorful blocks into a line. In this course, students are also introduced to the coding concept of *function*.

Essential Questions

> What makes a robot a robot?
> What is *tangible programming*, and how is it different from other computer programming languages?
> How do we write code that is "elegant"?

Learning Outcomes

During the course, students will:
> discuss and document the uses of the terms *tangible programming* and *elegant code*;
> explore the design, mechanics, and programming of the Primo robotics set and the KIBO robot;
> create increasingly complex and elegant code to program robots to perform specific tasks and actions;
> define and use computer programming terms and concepts, such as *code*, *symbol*, *sequence*, and *function*;
> use math and spatial reasoning skills to map and measure the paths of the robots; and
> compare and contrast the form and function of two kinds of robots, Primo and KIBO.

Materials

> Teacher's copies of read-aloud books (see Welcome Circle)
> Teacher resources (see Primo Pathways Resources section)
> Student copies of Robotics Assessment (see p. 156)
> 1 Primo Cubetto Playset
> 1 KIBO Kit
> Pegboard sets, blocks, cardboard, and/or other construction materials
> Different kinds of paper, writing and drawing materials, rulers, stencils, protractors, and/or examples of maps and algorithms
> Index cards, long strips of paper, string, and/or colored beads
> Images of robot "guts" and miscellaneous examples of robot parts (see Centers)
> Small screwdriver and extra batteries

LESSON PLANS AT A GLANCE

Monday	Tuesday	Wednesday	Thursday	Friday
Welcome Circle: Introductions. Read *If I Had a Robot.*	**Welcome Circle:** Read *Me on the Map* or *Follow that Map!*	**Welcome Circle:** Read *Robots* (Scholastic Reader).	**Welcome Circle:** Read *The Bot that Scott Built.*	**Welcome Circle:** Compare Primo to KIBO. Create final class story and plan for Expo.
Meet Mr. Cubetto	**Centers:** 1. Debugging and function (Primo Lessons 2–3) 2. Debugging and function (Primo Lessons 2–3) 3. Drafting: Design a disguise for Mr. Cubetto 4. Explore programming languages	**Meet KIBO**	**Centers:** 1. KIBO practice 2. Primo practice 3. Robot dissection 4. Explore programming languages	**Centers:** 1. Postassessment 2. Construction: Build a Primo/ KIBO pathway 3. Drafting: Map a Primo/KIBO pathway
Centers: 1. Preassessment 2. Construction: Pegboard patterns 3. Drafting: Make a map		**Centers:** 1. KIBO Moves (see KIBO Activity Guide) 2. Primo practice 3. Construction: Paths and roads for KIBO or Primo 4. Explore programming languages	**Recess/Break**	**Recess/Break**
Recess/Break	**Recess/Break**		**Revisit Centers**	**Prepare for Expo**
Centers: 1. Primo: Create an algorithm (Lessons 1–2) 2. Primo: Create an algorithm (Lessons 1–2) 3. Drafting: Draw a Primo path 4. Construction: Build a Primo path	**Revisit Centers**	**Recess/Break**	**Closing Circle:** Share one of the programming languages or stories invented today.	**Expo:** Present class story; display paths, maps, and codes; students teach parents how to program Primo and KIBO.
	Closing Circle: Share one of the programming languages or stories invented today.	**Revisit Centers**		
Closing Circle: Dictate a story about Mr. Cubetto.		**Closing Circle:** Dictate a KIBO story.		

LESSON DETAILS

Welcome Circle and Closing Circle

Welcome circle. Starting each class session with a welcome circle provides an opportunity to establish a sense of community, review the schedule and expectations, and take attendance. Students sit on the floor while the instructor leads the discussion. The instructor concludes the welcome circle with a read aloud of a storybook that relates to course content. Beginning each class with an engaging story helps young students make meaningful connections between the course content and their own feelings, experiences, and ideas. Students should also be encouraged to create their own stories, through writing, dictating, or pretending, as a way to organize and make sense of the new information they are learning in class. The important role of narrative in the Tech Beginnings curriculum is based on the theories of educators like Jerome Bruner (2002), who recognized that human beings need stories to connect to each other and to understand their world. Instructors may use any story that is related to the topics and ideas in the class. Try to choose books that tell a story with engaging characters and creative ideas, not just nonfiction books that describe course content. Suggested books include:

> *If I Had a Robot* **by Dan Yaccarino:** Discuss: What is a robot?
> *Me on the Map* **by Joan Sweeney** or *Follow That Map!: A First Book of Mapping Skills* **by Scot Ritchie:** Discuss: How do we get Mr. Cubetto from one place to another? What is code? What is an "elegant" code?
> *Robots* **(Scholastic Reader) by Gail Tuchman:** Discuss: What is tangible programming?
> *The Bot That Scott Built* **by Kim Norman:** Discuss: What is a robot made of? How does it work?

Closing circle. At the end of each class, a closing circle provides an opportunity to briefly share ideas and highlights from the day and make a plan or goal for the next day. If any students have written or dictated a story, that story can be shared with the group at the closing circle. This is also a good time to share interesting comments and questions from students or to show examples of new programming languages students have created (see the explore programming languages center).

Centers

Pre- and postassessment. The pre- and postassessments (see p. 156) are intended to measure and document students' general understanding of robots and computer programming. Students can draw or write their answers. The same handout can be used for both pre- and postassessment. Young students who are not fluent writers can be invited to dictate responses to an adult. In practice, it may be difficult to find classroom time for every student to dictate a response one-on-one with an adult. Instructors can try to collect as many responses as is reasonable in the time available. Another option might be to ask parents to write down students' postassessment responses at home or during Expo.

Construction/pegboard patterns. The construction center is an open-ended learning center where students can experiment with construction materials and ideas that are related to the Primo and KIBO robots. For example, on the first day of class, the construction center can be equipped with pegboard sets that are similar to the Primo pegboard where students will create sequences of code. Playing with pegboards may spark some ideas and conversations for the kinds of patterns and programming languages students will use in their computer code. On other days, the construction center can be equipped with blocks, cardboard, or other construction materials, and students can be encouraged to create 3-D structures for the robots, such as bridges the robots can travel over or under, or homes that can house the robots. At some point, students will likely discover that they will need to measure the robots in order to create constructions that fit their size. Students can be encouraged to use both standard and nonstandard units of measurement. Have rulers, measuring tape, graph paper, pens, and pencils ready for students to document their ideas and research.

Drafting. This center is for different kinds of drawing, writing, drafting, and mapping activities. Instructors may suggest tasks or challenges to be addressed in this center, but students should also have the opportunity to choose their own tasks to work on. The center should be equipped with different kinds of paper, writing and drawing materials, rulers, stencils, protractors, and examples of maps and algorithms. The materials can be rotated each day so there are always new materials or prompts to spark ideas.

Primo. One Primo Cubetto set is enough for one classroom. The wireless signals sometimes get crossed when using more than one in a single class. The instructor and/or teaching assistant should directly supervise the use of the Primo pegboard and Cubetto initially, but once students become familiar with how it works and have demonstrated that they can treat it with care, they can be allowed to work independently with the play sets at a learning center.

KIBO. The basic KIBO set comes with a limited number of programming blocks, as compared to Primo Cubetto. Because there are so few blocks, one of the challenges for writing KIBO code will be figuring out how to do a lot with very little. Initially, the instructor can suggest challenges, but students can also experiment. They will soon see how the repeat block on the KIBO has a similar function to the green peg in the Primo pegboard. Students can be encouraged to use critical thinking to compare the way the two robots, Primo and KIBO, function and the ways they can be programmed.

Explore programming languages. At this center students are challenged to come up with multiple ways to represent the codes that program the Primo and KIBO robots. Students will likely understand easily the idea that pegs (Primo) and the blocks (KIBO) make the robot respond in certain ways. But they will need a way to document or represent the code they are using to program the robots so they can remember what they have tried and continue to improve and refine their ideas. Explain to students that people communicate with robots through *computer code*. The creation of these codes is called *programming*. Codes can be written or recorded in many different ways. Each is a language. Some of the programming languages students can create and explore at this center include:

> drawing arrows on index cards, each card representing a peg or block in the interface;

> drawing arrows or symbols on a long strip of paper or on a grid;

> creating a sequence of hand signals to represent the commands in the code; and

> stringing colored beads, each color of bead representing a command.

Challenge students to come up with their own way of representing the code, their own programming language. Perhaps they will discover that sound can also be used as a programming language (a tap means go forward, a stomp means go back).

Robot dissection. Students may become curious about what is inside the Primo Cubetto robot or the KIBO robot. We don't recommend actually taking apart these valuable devices, but the "Robot Dissection Center" is where students can touch and explore the kinds of components used to create a functioning robot. This center can be equipped with images and diagrams that show what is inside the robots, as well as examples of wheels, switches, circuit boards, and computer chips. The user manual and DIY assembly guide on the Primo website (available at https://www.primotoys.com/resources/#usermanual) include illustrations showing the parts and workings of the Cubetto robot. Students can sketch these components or create (nonfunctioning) prototypes or models of the inside of a robot.

TEACHER PREPARATION

Teaching Primo, KIBO, and Programming Languages

Teaching students how to program a Primo Cubetto robot or a KIBO robot to follow increasingly complex paths will provide a foundation of programming knowledge and skills. Here is a description of suggested programming tasks, from the most simple to the more complex. You may find that there are other interesting tasks that will engage students in even more exciting learning experiences.

1. **Programming basics: How to use the command blocks/pegs (Primo) or command blocks (KIBO).** Briefly demonstrate and explain the use of each of the direction pegs: forward, left, and right (Primo), or forward, turn left, and turn right (KIBO). Some young students may not yet have a clear understanding of right and left. You may need to incorporate that concept into the introductory lessons.

2. **Teach the vocabulary for *symbol, code, sequence*, and *algorithm*:** Use simple and direct language to describe and define these concepts. A symbol is something that stands for something else, like a smiley face means happy. An arrow pointing forward is a symbol for moving forward. A code is what you create when you put symbols in a row, on paper or when you program a robot. A sequence is a bunch of symbols or commands in a row, one after another, on a page of paper or in time. An algorithm is a set of instructions.

3. **Spatial reasoning: Navigating on a grid.** In order to program a Primo or KIBO to move from point A to point B, you have to reason or think about the path the robot will take and translate that into a sequence of commands, or code. Students will need to predict, estimate, or measure distances in order to create their codes. One of the challenges most students will find is that a command to turn will only turn; it will not move the robot forward. Students will learn through experimentation, or trial and error, that turning and moving are two separate commands. One way to add complexity to this process is to put new obstacles in the path of the robot and challenge students to program the robot to navigate around the obstacles.

4. **Calibration and measurement:** At some point as students begin exploring what a robot can do, they will discover that the robots are *calibrated*. Every time the forward block is used, the robot moves forward exactly the same distance. Students will be challenged to measure and document what that distance is and incorporate that knowledge into

their coding. This should happen almost naturally as students explore what a robot can do. Be ready to facilitate that process with materials, such as big pieces of paper, rulers, and yardsticks, which can be used to document and measure the distances the robots travel.

5. **Using a function command to create more "elegant" code:** On the Primo pegboard, the commands placed in the function line can be represented by the green block. When the green block is placed in the sequence, students use one block to represent commands in the function line, thereby creating a more elegant code. The repeat loop in KIBO is similar to but not the same as the function line in Primo. The repeat loop allows the student to program the KIBO to repeat a command or sequence of commands. Both the function line and the repeat loops simulate the ways professional computer programmers create more refined, efficient, and elegant code.

6. **Programming languages:** As described in the explore programming languages center, every time students find a new way to represent their code, they have invented a new programming language. Use the closing circle at the end of each class session to share and demonstrate the different kinds of programming languages students have created and used each day.

Instructors are encouraged to use the publications provided by the manufacturers to help familiarize themselves with the functioning and programming of the Primo play sets and the KIBO robot. The Primo Cubetto lesson plans are available on the Primo Toys website at https://www.primotoys.com/resources/#lesson plan. KIBO curriculum resources are available on the Early Childhood Robotics Network website at http://tkroboticsnetwork.ning.com/page/curric-starters.

IDEAS FOR DIFFERENTIATION

The structure of the lessons, with opportunities to explore a variety of learning centers, is designed to allow students to learn and explore at their own pace. Students who need more time to master new ideas can be allowed to spend a longer amount of time in a learning center, or be allowed to make their own choice for which center to visit, as long as that strategy does not disrupt the rest of the classroom.

For students needing greater challenge, here are some suggestions:

> **Programming languages:** Challenge advanced students to come up with programming languages that are completely different from those used in class. A student who plays a musical instrument could create a

piece of music in which specific notes or sounds represent specific commands or codes.

> **Mapping:** Students with advanced spatial reasoning skills could be challenged to create accurate maps of the various paths students have created or imagined. They could add map features, such as a compass rose or a key to scale.

> **Documenting with words, images, audio, and video:** A student who is reluctant to participate could be tasked with documenting the class's progress. He or she could write a story, take photos, or make a recording of the robots and/or students. Students could also be challenged to write or dictate fiction about the robots, imagining their personalities and adventures.

> **Right angles and measuring angles:** A student with advanced math ability could be challenged to explore and measure the angles involved in robot movements and programming. Each turn of a robot is a right angle, which is 90 degrees. Introduce the student to the concept of angles and that angles can be measured by degrees. Ask: If a circle is 360 degrees, how many degrees is a right angle? How many degrees does the robot travel if it turns right twice? A protractor could be introduced as a tool for measuring angles.

> **Critical thinking:** Challenge advanced students to think about how the robots fit into the broader world of robots and computer programming. Ask: Which do you like better, the Primo or the KIBO? Why? How could you improve on the functioning or design of these robots? If you could build your own robot, what would it look like? How would you program it?

The KIBO curriculum resources available through the Early Childhood Robotics Network (http://tkroboticsnetwork.ning.com/page/curric-starters) include many lessons and activities that could be adapted to challenge a student or a group of students who are ready to consider more advanced robotics concepts.

PRIMO PATHWAYS RESOURCES

> Primo Education (available at https://www.primotoys.com/education)
> Primo lesson plans (available at https://www.primotoys.com/resources/#lessonplan)
> KinderLab Robotics (available at http://kinderlabrobotics.com)
> KIBO curricula (available at http://kinderlabrobotics.com/curricula)
> KIBO curriculum resources (available at http://tkroboticsnetwork.ning.com/page/curric-starters)

UNIT III
Hexbug Habitats

COURSE DESCRIPTION

Hexbug toys are a fascinating example of bio-inspired robotics, the study of how to make robots simulate living organisms. Students analyze the form and function of various Hexbug creatures and build habitats that demonstrate each robot's unique characteristics.

Essential Questions

> Are Hexbugs more like robots or more like toys?
> What can bugs teach us about robotic engineering?
> How does a robotic sensor work?

Learning Outcomes

During the course, students will:
> research and explore the concept of *bio-robotics* and *bio-inspired robotics*;
> explore the design, mechanics, and programming of Hexbug robotic toys;
> conduct experiments and research, such as taking apart Hexbugs, that demonstrate the purpose and function of robotic sensors;
> build roads, mazes, and obstacle courses for Hexbugs; and
> evaluate the form and function of Hexbugs and test them for speed and durability.

Materials

> Teacher's copies of read-aloud books (see Welcome Circle)
> Teacher resources (see Hexbug Habitats Resources section)
> Student copies of Robotics Assessment (see p. 156)
> Hexbugs (recommended: Nanos, Scarabs, Ants, Larva, Spider, AquaBots)

> Cubelets
> Fishbowl
> Extra batteries
> Insect books, images, videos, and specimens (see Centers)
> LEGOs, blocks
> Small screwdrivers

LESSON PLANS AT A GLANCE

Monday	Tuesday	Wednesday	Thursday	Friday
Welcome Circle: Introductions. Read *Eight Legs Up*.	**Welcome Circle:** Read *The Foot Book* and watch slow motion video.	**Welcome Circle:** Read *Road Builders*.	**Welcome Circle:** Read *Swimmy*. Introduce AquaBots and the concept of sensors.	**Welcome Circle:** Create a plan for Expo.
Introduce Hexbugs	**Centers:** Hexbug challenges:	**Centers:** Habitats:		**Postassessment in Centers:**
Preassessment in Centers: How do Hexbugs move?	1. Nano	1. Nano mazes out of LEGOs	**Centers:** Sensors and programming:	1. Nano
1. Nano	2. Hexbug surgery	2. Scarab mazes out of blocks	1. Test AquaBots in water	2. Scarab
2. Scarab	3. Scarab	3. Ant obstacle course	2. Cubelets: Construct a Cubelet robot with a light or motion sensor and/or Experiment with Ozobot	3. Ant
3. Ant	4. Ant	4. Larva surface challenge	3. Hexbug hospital/ Hexbug morgue	4. Larva
4. Larva	5. Larva	5. Spider maps	4. Open construction site	5. Spider
5. Spider	6. Spider			
Recess/Break	**Recess/Break**	**Recess/Break**	**Recess/Break**	**Recess/Break**
Centers: Research. Introduce *bio-inspired robotics*. Compare Hexbugs to real bugs.	**Revisit Centers**	**Revisit Centers**	**Revisit Centers**	**Prepare for Expo:** Create tracks for a Hexbug Race.
1. Books	**Closing Circle:** Hexbug charades.	**Closing Circle:** Share images, ideas, or narratives from habitat centers	**Closing Circle:** Create a class story about AquaBots.	**Expo:** Present class projects; display student work; conduct Hexbug races.
2. Images				
3. Video				
4. Observe real insects				
Closing Circle: Hexbug charades.				

LESSON DETAILS

Welcome Circle and Closing Circle

Welcome circle. Starting each class session with a welcome circle provides an opportunity to establish a sense of community, review the schedule and expectations, and take attendance. Students sit on the floor while the instructor leads the discussion. The instructor concludes the welcome circle with a read aloud of a picture book that relates to course content. Beginning each class with an engaging story helps young students make meaningful connections between the course content and their own feelings, experiences, and ideas. Students should also be encouraged to create their own stories, through writing, dictating, or pretending, as a way to organize and make sense of the new information they are learning in class. The important role of narrative in the Tech Beginnings curriculum is based on the theories of educators like Jerome Bruner (2002), who recognized that human beings need stories to connect to each other and to understand their world. Instructors may use any story that is related to the topics and ideas in the class. Try to choose books that tell a story with engaging characters and creative ideas, not just nonfiction books that describe course content. Suggested books include:

> *Eight Legs Up* **by David Kirk:** Discuss: How do bugs move?
> *The Foot Book: Dr. Seuss's Wacky Book of Opposites* **by Dr. Seuss:** Discuss: How does the design of a Hexbug leg or foot affect the way it moves? What can bugs teach us about robotic engineering? If possible, also show one of the slow-motion videos listed in this unit's resource section.
> *Road Builders* **by B. G. Hennessy:** Discuss: What kind of road or home would you build for a Hexbug?
> *Swimmy* **by Leo Lionni:** Discuss: Can a robot see or feel or smell? Why or why not?

Closing circle. At the end of each class, a closing circle provides an opportunity to briefly share ideas and highlights from the day and make a plan or goal for the next day. If any students have written or dictated a story or narrative, it can be shared with the group at the closing circle. Students can also participate in Hexbug charades, which provides them an opportunity to kinesthetically demonstrate what they've learned about the form and function of the Hexbugs. Students can take turns moving like one of the Hexbugs and having the rest of the students guess which Hexbug they are imitating.

Centers

Pre- and postassessment. The pre- and postassessments (see p. 156) are intended to measure and document students' general understanding of robots and computer programming. Students can draw or write their answers. The same handout can be used for both pre- and postassessment. Young students who are not fluent writers can be invited to dictate responses to an adult. In practice, it may be difficult to find classroom time for every student to dictate a response one-on-one with an adult. Instructors can try to collect as many responses as is reasonable in the time available. Another option might be to ask parents to write down students' postassessment responses at home or during Expo.

Research. Introduce bio-inspired robotics and compare Hexbugs to real bugs. Invite students to compare Hexbugs to real bugs. Because time is short, each student should probably focus on one type of Hexbug, either Nano (cockroach), Scarab (beetle), Ant (ant), Larva (young beetle or fly), or Spider (spider). See "Teaching Hexbugs and Cubelets" in the Teacher Preparation section for more information.

1. Research centers allow students to use a variety of media and sources to conduct their research. Students should rotate through the centers and record their ideas and observations in a journal or notebook.
2. Materials at the research centers may include:
   ▶ **Books:** A variety of nonfiction books about insects.
   ▶ **Images:** Digital or paper images of the insects.
   ▶ **Video:** Preselected videos from YouTube and other sources.
   ▶ **Observe real insects:** Observe preserved insect samples. Insect specimens are available for purchase through science education suppliers, such as Nasco (https://www.enasco.com/product/SB48191M).

Hexbug challenges. Invite students to work on Hexbug challenges in centers. Each challenge is designed to inspire students to think carefully about the form and function of each Hexbug. In each center, students are asked to make a prediction about what will happen if we "hack" or change the Hexbug in some way. Then, students will have the opportunity to observe what happens and then compare their prediction to the actual outcome. Depending on which types of Hexbugs are available, students can rotate through centers, such as:

1. **Nano:** How will a Nano move when it has no legs?
2. **Hexbug surgery:** What will we find inside of a Hexbug?
3. **Scarab:** What will happen if we flip a Scarab over onto its back?
4. **Ant:** What will happen if we attach a weight to the ant's antennae?
5. **Larva:** What will happen if we tape the tail of the larva so it can't wiggle?
6. **Spider:** What will happen if we change channels on the Spider (from A to B or from B to A)?

Habitats. Each center should be stocked with construction materials that will allow for open-ended exploration:

1. **Nano mazes out of LEGOs:** Students construct mazes out of LEGOs (examples in videos listed in the Resources section of this unit).

2. **Scarab mazes out of blocks:** Students use blocks to create paths and mazes for the Hexbug Scarab.

3. **Ant obstacle course**: Students use a variety of objects and construction materials to create an obstacle course that an ant (with its useful antennae) would be able to successfully navigate.

4. **Larva surface challenge:** Students can test out various surfaces to observe how the surface affects the speed and path of the Hexbug. Surfaces can include those found in the classroom, such as tile or carpet, as well as a variety of other kinds of materials, such as fabric or metal. Students can also experiment with whether the Hexbug can handle an incline.

5. **Spider maps:** Navigate the spider on a large piece of paper and map its path using markers and rulers. Challenge students to find a way to perhaps attach a marker or crayon to the Spider so that it records its own path.

Sensors and programming. Introduce AquaBots and the concept of sensors. Demonstrate how an AquaBot will begin swimming once it is placed in water. Ask: How does the AquaBot know it is time to turn on and start swimming? Students should rotate through four centers:

1. **Test Aquabots in water:** Students should observe and play with the Aquabots in a bowl or bin filled with water. If there are enough Aquabots, two centers can be equipped with AquaBots. See "Teaching Hexbugs and Cubelets" in the Teacher Preparation section for more information.

2. **Cubelets:** Construct a Cubelet robot with a light or motion sensor. One of the simplest constructions is the "Dud Light," a three-block structure that includes the battery cube (power), the brightness cube (senses light), and the flashlight cube. When students are assigned to this center, they can build the Dud Light and test it by dimming the available light under a cloth. Students who enjoy the challenge of building with Cubelets can be invited to build other structures. See "Teaching Hexbugs and Cubelets" in the Teacher Preparation section for more information.

3. **Hexbug hospital/Hexbug morgue:** Some Hexbugs will have likely died or are broken. Students can work on reviving these Hexbugs with new batteries, or they can conduct autopsies by taking apart the "dead" Hexbugs.

4. **Open construction site:** In this open-ended learning center, students can use blocks or LEGOs to create any kind of path or habitat for a Hexbug.

TEACHER PREPARATION

Teaching Hexbugs and Cubelets

The term *bio-inspired robotics* is used in the course description to describe robots, such as Hexbugs, that simulate living organisms. Note that the term *bio-robotics* (or *biorobotics*, depending on your fondness for hyphens) has a different meaning—it is used most often in the field of medicine to describe research and programs that incorporate robotics to heal or help the human body. Hexbugs are actually closer to the family of *bio-inspired robotics* than *bio-robotics*. Background information about both *bio-robotics* and *bio-inspired robotics* can be found in the Resources section of this unit.

For the purposes of this course, students should be introduced to both terms, *bio-robotics* and *bio-inspired robotics*. We suggest explaining to students that *bio-robotics* is a field in medicine and health care and informs, for example, how an artificial hand might be designed. *Bio-inspired robotics* is a field in engineering and informs, for example, how a robotic rover might move across the surface of Mars. We suggest instructors save the AquaBots until Thursday when the lesson will focus on the use of sensors. AquaBots are a special kind of Hexbug. They are fish, not insects, so they travel through water. They also have sensors.

Cubelets are another kind of robotic toy/kit that uses sensors. More information about using Cubelets is available online at http://www.modrobotics.com/cubelets and on the package inserts.

On the last day of class, in addition to the postassessment activity, a suggested activity is to create a Hexbug racetrack or obstacle course and conduct a big race or contest to show off the Hexbugs for the parents and visitors. This would also be a good opportunity for students to reflect on the strengths and weaknesses of the different models of Hexbugs and perhaps create their own design for a Hexbug.

IDEAS FOR DIFFERENTIATION

The structure of the lessons, with opportunities to explore a variety of learning centers, is designed to allow students to learn and explore at their own pace. Students who need more time to master new ideas can be allowed to spend a longer amount of time in a learning center, or be allowed to make their own choice for which center to visit, as long as that strategy does not disrupt the rest of the classroom.

For students needing greater challenge, here are some suggestions:

> **Documenting with words, images, audio, and video:** A student who is reluctant to participate could be tasked with documenting the class's progress. He or she could write a story, take photos, or make a recording of the Hexbugs and/or students. Students could also be challenged to write or dictate fiction about the Hexbugs, imagining their personalities and adventures.
> **Build and program with Cubelets:** Students needing an additional challenge can be invited to experiment with the Cubelets. The set of Cubelet blocks can be used to create structures or "robots" from the very simple to the very complex. They are also compatible with LEGOs, so many design features can be built onto the cubes with LEGOs. See the Cubelets website (listed in Hexbug Habitats Resources) for more information.
> **Hack the Hexbugs:** Students needing an additional challenge can also be encouraged to "hack" the design of the Hexbugs to create their own kind of creature. Lightweight materials such as wire and paper can be attached to a Hexbug to alter the appearance and the movements of the Hexbug.
> **Evaluate the Hexbugs:** Students with a lot of experience and prior knowledge about Hexbugs can be encouraged to create their own Hexbug design and send their ideas and feedback to the Hexbug company using the contact information found on the website.

HEXBUG HABITATS RESOURCES

> Hexbug (available at https://www.hexbug.com)
> Cubelets Education (available at http://www.modrobotics.com/education)
> Bio-inspired robotics resources:

- ▶ Wyss Institute: Autonomous Flying Microbots (RoboBees) (available at http://wyss.harvard.edu/technology/autonomous-flying-microbots-robobees)
- ▶ Bio-inspired robotics video (available at https://vimeo.com/15739182)
- ▶ "Bugs and Bots Enthrall at Ed Portal" (available at http://www.thecrimson.com/article/2011/2/4/finio-kids-bugs-robots)
- ▶ "Channeling Your Inner Entomologist" (available at http://static.nsta.org/files/sc1409_28.pdf)
- ▶ "Hexbugs-Robot Toys Mimic Animals" (available at http://singularityhub.com/2009/09/23/hexbugs-robot-toys-mimic-animals-videos)
- ▶ Festo BionicANTs (available at https://www.festo.com/group/en/cms/10157.htm)

> Video resources:
  - ▶ "The Sticky Wonder of Gecko Feet" (available at https://www.ted.com/talks/robert_full_on_animal_movement)
  - ▶ "3-D X-ray Provides Detailed Images of How Living Insects Move" (available at https://www.youtube.com/watch?v=sGsbUDwO1F4)
  - ▶ Insects and animals in slow motion:
    - "Walking Ant in Slow-Motion" (available at https://www.youtube.com/watch?v=IHEYBvriv2I)
    - "Insect Flight in Slow Motion" (available at https://www.youtube.com/watch?v=DlF91R41Pso)
    - "Fastest Animals on Earth in Slow Motion-Animal Camera-BBC" (available at https://www.youtube.com/watch?v=zcWxAfl0okE)

  - ▶ Hexbug mazes:
    - "LEGO Hexbug Maze With 5 Hexbugs" (available at https://www.youtube.com/watch?v=lVnUWDv5S7g)
    - "LEGO Maze for Hex Bug Nano 2010" (available at https://www.youtube.com/watch?v=7j5VnM6375M)
    - "Hex Bug LEGO Maze" (available at https://www.youtube.com/watch?v=4DXYsw_uD4U)

  - ▶ "Can a Hex Bug Fish Swim in the Sea??? Aquabot Swimming Test Review Micro Robotic Robot" (available at https://www.youtube.com/watch?v=HFd1vDe8cwc)
  - ▶ "Can a Hex Bug Fish Swim in Chocolate Syrup?? Aquabot Swimming Test Review Micro Robotic Robot" (available at https://www.youtube.com/watch?v=4ag7DWwrQks)

> Picture books related to Hexbugs, insects, machines, toys, or bio-robotics
- *The Beautiful Beetle Book* by Sue Unstead (Nonfiction, lift-the-flap book)
- *Bug Off!: Creepy Crawly Poems* by Jane Yolen (Praying Mantis on pp. 8–9 looks like a robotic arm)
- *Bugs A to Z* by Scholastic (Nonfiction reference book)
- *Cockroach* by Karen Hartley
- *Color and Noise!: Let's Play With Toys!* by Janice Lobb
- *Creepy, Crawly Jokes About Spiders and Other Bugs* by Melissa Stewart
- *Eight Legs Up* by David Kirk (How the number of your legs affects what you can do well)
- *Flit, Flutter, Fly!* edited by Lee Bennett Hopkins
- *The Foot Book* by Dr. Seuss (Whimsical look at all different kinds of feet)
- *How Toys Spin* by Helen Whittaker
- *Insect Bodies*, A Bobbie Kalman Book (Nonfiction, looks at backbones, body sections, eyes, antennae, legs, wings)
- *Leo Cockroach, Toy Tester* by Kevin O'Malley
- *The Magic School Bus Explores the World of Bugs*
- *Making Things Move* by Dustyn Roberts
- *Martina the Beautiful Cockroach* by Carmen Agra Deedy
- *Miss Spider's Tea Party* by David Kirk (Rhyming picture book about a spider and her insect friends)
- *Nasty Bugs: Poems* Edited by Lee Bennett Hopkins
- *Pull, Lift, and Lower: A Book About Pulleys* by Michael Dahl (Nonfiction, simple machines)
- *Roadbuilders* by B. G. Hennessy (Beautifully illustrated picture book about the big machines that make roads)
- *Simple Machines* by Allan Fowler
- *Simple Machines* by Rebecca Rissman
- *Swimmy* by Leo Lionni

UNIT IV
WeDo Go

COURSE DESCRIPTION

Students will build and program simple robots using LEGO WeDo robotics kits. This course provides an introductory pathway to more advanced LEGO robotics experiences. Although this course is designed for children in second grade, these lesson plans also include options for differentiation that allow for scaffolding for third graders.

Essential Questions

> What do engineers need to know to build and program a robot?
> Which is more important, how a robot is constructed or how a robot is programmed?
> How is a robot like a human being? How is it different?
> Do robots make the world a better a place? Why or why not?

Learning Outcomes

During the course, students will:
> engage in critical thinking and discussions to determine a definition of the term *robot*;
> build and program at least two WeDo robot projects;
> explore and practice block programming to create increasingly complex codes;
> observe, analyze, and document the mechanical structures of robots; and
> write, dictate, or perform individual or group stories, fiction or nonfiction, which explore the relationships between humans and robots.

103

Materials

> Teacher's copies of read-aloud books (see Welcome Circle)
> 2–3 WeDo kits (one kit per pair of students at the center)
> 4–6 iPads and/or computers compatible with WeDo software (available at https://education.lego.com/en-us/downloads/wedo) and Blockly (available at https://developers.google.com/blockly)
> 4–6 iPads or video cameras for movie project (see Centers)
> Rubber robot toy, iPod or iPhone, toy robotic arm, and electric can opener for preassessment
> LEGOs and mini-figures for free building

LESSON PLANS AT A GLANCE

Monday	Tuesday	Wednesday	Thursday	Friday
Welcome Circle: Introductions and read *Robots Slither*.	**Welcome Circle:** Read *The Most Magnificent Thing*.	**Welcome Circle:** Read *Hello, Robots!*	**Welcome Circle:** Read *My Truck Is Stuck!*	**Welcome Circle:** Create final class story and plan for Expo.
Preassessment Centers: 1. A rubber robot toy 2. An iPod 3. A robotic arm 4. An electric can opener	**WeDo Project 1:** Begin building Dancing Birds.	**WeDo Project 1:** Begin/continue programming.	**WeDo Project 4:** Program Hungry Alligator.	**Postassessment Centers:** 1. Write a definition of "robot" 2. Create a programming language for Expo 3. Create a Venn diagram comparing robots and people 4. Write or draw an evil robot story
Recess/Break	**Recess/Break**	**Recess/Break**	**Recess/Break**	
Introduce Block Programming	**WeDo Project 1:** Continue building, or, if time permits, begin programming.	**WeDo Project 4:** Begin building Hungry Alligator.	**Finish Project 4**	
Centers: 1. Explore Blockly 2. Explore an example of WeDo code 3. Construction: Build with LEGOs 4. Drafting: Design a robot	**Closing Circle:** Dictate a class story about the Dancing Birds.	**Centers:** 1. Explore Blockly 2. Construct a home for the birds or alligator 3. Write or draw an alligator story 4. Make a WeDo movie	**Centers:** 1. Explore Blockly 2. Construct a home for the birds or alligator 3. Write or draw an alligator story 4. Make a WeDo movie	**Recess/Break**
				Prepare for Expo
Closing Circle: Dictate a class robot story.		**Closing Circle:** Share or dictate a robot story.	**Closing Circle:** Share or dictate a robot story.	**Expo:** Present class story; display robots; students teach parents how to program using block programming.

LESSON DETAILS

Welcome Circle and Closing Circle

Welcome circle. Starting each class session with a welcome circle provides an opportunity to establish a sense of community, review the schedule and expectations, and take attendance. Students sit on the floor while the instructor leads the discussion. The instructor concludes the welcome circle with a read aloud of a storybook that relates to course content.

Beginning each class with an engaging story helps young students make meaningful connections between the course content and their own feelings, experiences, and ideas. Students should also be encouraged to create their own stories, through writing, dictating, or pretending, as a way to organize and make sense of the new information they are learning in class. The important role of narrative in the Tech Beginnings curriculum is based on the theories of educators like Jerome Bruner (2002), who recognized that human beings need stories to connect to each other and to understand their world. Instructors may use any story that is related to the topics and ideas in the class. Choose books that tell a story with engaging characters and creative ideas, not just nonfiction books that describe course content. Suggested books include:

> - ***Robots Slither* by Ryan Ann Hunter:** Discuss: What is a robot?
> - ***Hello, Robots!* by Bob Staake:** Discuss: What can go wrong with robots?
> - ***The Most Magnificent Thing* by Ashley Spires:** Discuss the concept of *iterations*. Engineers often build multiple iterations before they find a design that will work.
> - ***My Truck Is Stuck!* by Kevin Lewis and Daniel Kirk:** Discuss: How do machines make things move?

Closing circle. At the end of each class, a closing circle provides an opportunity to briefly share ideas and highlights from the day and make a plan or goal for the next day. If any students have written or dictated a story, that story can be shared with the group at the closing circle, or, if time permits, the group could dictate a story together. This is also a good time to share interesting comments and questions from students.

WeDo Projects

Students should focus on two WeDo projects, Dancing Birds and Hungry Alligator. For details, see "Teaching WeDo Robotics" in the Teacher Preparation section (p. 108).

Centers

Pre- and postassessments. The pre- and postassessments are intended to measure and document students' general understanding of robots and computer programming. The preassessment activity is intended to both promote and measure students' critical thinking about what makes a robot a robot. At each learning center students should be presented with an object and asked to consider whether or not the object is a robot. Students should rotate through four centers and complete an assessment at each (see Figure 5):

1. a rubber robot toy,
2. an iPod or iPhone,
3. a toy robotic arm, and
4. an electric can opener.

After students have an opportunity to visit each center, the instructor should collect the assessments and lead a discussion in which students create a class list of "characteristics of robots." This list can be added to or edited as the course progresses.

On the last day of class, students should participate in four postassessment activities in centers:

1. Write a definition of "robot."
2. Create a programming language.
3. Create a Venn diagram comparing robots and people.
4. Write or draw a robot story.

Explore Blockly. There are a number of websites that offer online games that introduce students to block programming. One favorite is Blockly. The center should be set up with 4–5 computers with the Blockly website already selected and loaded. Students will likely be able to work through the games on their own. Later, when students have had some experience with the WeDo programming, the instructor may want to initiate a discussion about the similarities and differences between block programming in Blockly and block programming in WeDo. They are all part of the block programming family, but the appearance and functioning of the blocks are a little different in each platform.

Explore an example of WeDo code. This center demonstrates what WeDo code looks like and how it functions. If instructors have prior experience with WeDo, instructors should set up this center with one or two completed WeDo projects, preferably different ones from the two that will be created in this class. The robots should be hooked up to the computer so students can see the code at work. Students should have an opportunity to simply play with robots by activating the code that is already written for the projects on display. Instructors may

Name: _____ Date: _____

WEDO GO PREASSESSMENT
What Is a Robot?

Is this a robot? Why or why not?

_____

_____

_____

_____

Figure 5. Sample WeDo Go preassessment.

want to ask students to sketch the robot or write down the code on paper, as ways to draw students' attention to characteristics of the robots and the codes. If a finished WeDo project is not available for demonstration, an alternative activity is to show a YouTube video made by WeDo users, such as https://www.youtube.com/watch?v=ph1GtstVgas.

Construction. The construction center can be a place for open-ended construction with LEGOs or a place to build accessories or homes for the birds or alligators being created in the course. Our experience has been that, in LEGO robotics courses, students often need time to just mess around with the materials and have fun with LEGOs bricks.

Write or draw an alligator story. This learning center should be equipped with a variety of drawing and writing materials, such as graph paper, lined paper, drawing paper, pencils and pens, rulers, and stencils. Instructors can choose to leave this center open-ended and allow students to choose what they want to create, or offer a content-related challenge, such as design a robot or create an alligator story.

Make a WeDo movie. On the third and fourth days of class, after some of the projects have been built and programmed, students can be invited to capture the work of the class in video or images, depending on what types of cameras are available. Students who are assigned to this learning center should also document their filming process so the work has some structure and organization. For example, the instructor can direct students at this center to make a list and agree on what they want to film and then use that list to conduct the filming. Students can be encouraged to create a narration or text to go with their film. Students should be limited on the length of each clip so that the footage is easier to share or edit later. Some of this footage could be shared with parents.

TEACHER PREPARATION

Teaching WeDo Robotics

The WeDo robotics kits come with software and teaching guides that demonstrate a clear sequence for teachers to use when working with students to build and program each of the WeDo projects (*Note.* This unit was developed using WeDo 1.0 kits and software). In this unit, the primary goal is to introduce students to the general structure of LEGO robotics, the broad concept of block programming, and some critical thinking about the role of robots in our world. Our expectation is that students will only have time to build two projects. The suggested projects in this course are Projects 1 and 4—the dancing birds and the hungry alligator. Instructors are free to choose other projects to replace or supplement this lesson plan.

IDEAS FOR DIFFERENTIATION

The structure of the lessons, with opportunities to explore a variety of learning centers, is designed to allow students to learn and explore at their own pace. Students who need more time to master new ideas can be allowed to spend a longer amount of time in a learning center, or be allowed to make their own choice for which center to visit, as long as that strategy does not disrupt the rest of the classroom.

For students needing greater challenge, here are some suggestions:

> **Explore other programming platforms:** If students are particularly interested in programming, and need a challenge beyond the WeDo programming, they can be encouraged to explore other kinds of block programming through the variety of "Hour of Code" tutorials at Code.org.

> **Build other projects in the WeDo curriculum:** If students are able to quickly build and program the class projects, allow them to move on to

other projects at their own pace. The kits should allow for at least eight total projects.

> **Invent your own original WeDo projects:** If students are frustrated by the specificity of the WeDo projects and would like to adapt or change the projects to make their own robots, they should be allowed to do so. Students can be encouraged to document their projects with instructions that can be shared with other students.

> **Advocate for change:** Students who are especially frustrated or creative can also be encouraged to write down their feedback about the WeDo kits and send their feedback to LEGO. Ask the student, "If you were a LEGO designer, what would you put in these kits?"

> **Explore other WeDo curricula:** LEGO Education provides a searchable library of robotics lesson plans at https://education.lego.com/en-us/lessons.

TRACK IV
Robot Quest (Program Your Own Adventure)

TRACK DESCRIPTION

Tech Beginnings robotics courses teach students the essential characteristics of robots: They are machines with a motor and a power source (such as electricity), are programmed by a computer or an internal or external computer chip or circuit, and perform a task or function. Students engage in "tangible programming" using robotic devices and physical objects they can move, manipulate, and hold to create computer code. Along the way, students also create stories, solve problems, and play games that deepen understanding of computer science and engineering concepts.

The units are:

Robot Chase: Grades Pre-K–K

Learn to program educational robots, such as Bee-Bots and robotic mice, to follow a path or run a race. Students practice and demonstrate introductory coding concepts, such as *symbol*, *sequence*, and *algorithm*, as they build spatial reasoning skills.

Robot Shortcut: Grades K–1

In the world of coding, a "function" is a shortcut that allows programmers to make their code shorter, more efficient, or more elegant. In the world of robots, educational devices like the Primo Cubetto and KIBO robots teach students how to use a function command to help their robot friends take a quick shortcut on their way to fun adventures.

Robot Reaction: Grades 1–2

How do we tell robots what to do? We give them commands, in the form of code. Some robots also have sensors that allow them to see, hear, or sense their environment. In this course, young robotic engineers learn to code educational robots like Ozobots and Hexbugs as they observe and analyze how sensors enhance a robot's functioning.

Robot Games: Grade 2

Exciting new tangible devices like Sphero, Cubelets, and Bloxels allow young, curious students to learn about both coding and robotic engineering. This course introduces coding, engineering, and spatial reasoning concepts, as well as game design. Students will use robotic and coding tools to create games that demonstrate design elements such as victory conditions and storylines.

UNIT I
Robot Chase

COURSE DESCRIPTION

Students will learn to program educational robots, such as Bee-Bots and robotic mice, to follow a path or run a race. Students practice and demonstrate introductory coding concepts, such as *symbol*, *sequence*, and *algorithm*, as they build spatial reasoning skills.

Essential Questions

> What is a robot?
> What is code?
> How do we use code to program robots?

Learning Outcomes

During the course, students will:
> discuss and document the uses of the term *robot*;
> explore the design, mechanics, and programming of robots;
> create increasingly complex codes to program robots to perform specific tasks and actions;
> define and use computer programming terms and concepts, such as *code*, *symbol*, and *sequence*;
> collaborate with classmates to create stories using words, images, construction materials, dramatic play, and robots; and
> map and measure landmarks that the robots must navigate as they move to programmed positions on a grid.

Materials

> Teacher's copies of read-aloud books (see Welcome Circle)
> Suggested videos (see Closing Circle)

> Student copies of Robotics Assessment (see p. 156)
> At least 6–8 Bee-Bots and charging station and/or charging cords
> Code & Go Robot Mouse (2–3 per center) and/or Fisher-Price Think & Learn Code-a-pillar (1 per center)
> Extra batteries (AA and AAA)
> Blocks, cardboard, and Straws and Connectors
> Model Magic, clay, or dough
> Hardware, such as nuts, bolts, washers, wire, or bottle caps
> Graph paper, pencils, markers, etc., for drafting
> Peaceable Kingdom The Great Cheese Chase game
> Peaceable Kingdom Race to the Treasure! game

LESSON PLANS AT A GLANCE

Monday	Tuesday	Wednesday	Thursday	Friday
Welcome Circle: Introductions and read *Robots, Robots Everywhere*.	**Welcome Circle:** Read *The Merry Chase*.	**Welcome Circle:** Read *The Great Gracie Chase*.	**Welcome Circle:** Read *Rosie's Walk*.	**Welcome circle:** Read *Robot Rumpus!*
Mini-Lesson: Meet the Bee-Bots.	**Mini-Lesson:** How can we represent our code?	**Mini-Lesson:** Synchronization.	**Mini-Lesson:** Calibration, measurement, and maps.	**Mini-Lesson:** Compare Bee-Bots to other robots.
Centers: 1. Preassessment 2. Bee-Bots 3. Construction 4. Clay robots	**Centers:** 1. Bee-Bots 2. Construction 3. Drafting 4. Games	**Centers:** 1. Bee-Bots 2. Construction 3. Drafting 4. Games	**Centers:** 1. Bee-Bots 2. Construction 3. Drafting 4. Games	**Centers:** 1. Postassessment 2. Robot mice 3. Code-a-pillar 4. Bee-Bots
Recess/Break	**Recess/Break**	**Recess/Break**	**Recess/Break**	**Recess/Break**
Revisit Centers	**Revisit Centers**	**Revisit Centers**	**Revisit Centers**	**Prepare for Expo**
Closing Circle: Video clip.	**Closing Circle:** Video clip.	**Closing Circle:** Video clip.	**Closing Circle:** Video clip	**Expo:** Display student work; students teach parents how to use the Bee-Bots.

LESSON DETAILS

Welcome Circle and Closing Circle

Welcome circle. Starting each class session with a welcome circle provides an opportunity to establish a sense of community, review the schedule and expectations, and take attendance. Students sit on the floor while the instructor leads the discussion. The instructor concludes the welcome circle with a read aloud of a storybook related to course concepts. Suggested books include:

> ***Robots, Robots Everywhere!* by Sue Fliess:** Discuss: What is a robot? What do you already know about robots? Have you ever seen a real robot? What robots in this book could be real, and which ones are pretend or imaginary?

> ***The Merry Chase* by Clement Hurd:** This book is an example of a simple storybook that can be used to talk about spatial reasoning and orientation. Discuss: Where does this story take place? How far did the cat and dog travel? How do you know? Students can also be challenged to act out the story, create a map of the story, or program the Bee-Bots to act out the story.

> ***The Great Gracie Chase: Stop That Dog!* by Cynthia Rylant:** This book, like *The Merry Chase*, can also be used to inspire discussion, play, mapping, and programming.

> ***Rosie's Walk* by Pat Hutchins:** This book can also be used to inspire discussion, play, mapping, and programming.

> ***Robot Rumpus!* by Sean Taylor:** Discuss: How are these robots like Bee-Bots? How are they different? What are robots good at? What can go wrong with robots?

Closing circle. At the end of each class, revisit one of the storybooks, reflect on student projects, or show and discuss a video clip about robots. Suggested videos include:

> "The Animatronic Animals of Spy in the Wild" (available at http://the kidshouldseethis.com/post/the-animatronic-animals-of-spy-in-the-wild)

> "Octopus, Elephant, & Human Arm Robot Assistants From Festo" (available at http://thekidshouldseethis.com/post/octopus-elephant-human-arm-robot-assistants-from-festo)

> "Tom & Jerry Bee-Bots Video" (available at https://www.youtube.com/watch?v=gMakAdTj6Zw)

> "Boston Dynamics' New SpotMini Robot" (available at http://thekid-shouldseethis.com/post/boston-dynamics-new-spotmini-robot)

> "Ultra Fast Robots Pick & Place Batteries to Form Group Patterns" (available at http://thekidshouldseethis.com/post/two-ultra-fast-robots-pick-place-batteries-to-form-group-patterns)

Mini-Lessons

See "Teaching Bee-Bots and Programming Languages" in the Teacher Preparation section (p. 117) for information about how to introduce the Bee-Bots and teach specific concepts. Any large-group lessons should be brief. Students will have the opportunity to practice the concepts in learning centers.

Centers

Pre- and postassessment. The pre- and postassessments (see p. 156) are intended to measure and document students' general understanding of robots and computer programming. Students can draw or write their answers. The same handout can be used for both pre- and postassessment. Young students who are not fluent writers can be invited to dictate responses to an adult. In practice, it may be difficult to find classroom time for every student to dictate a response one-on-one with an adult. Instructors can try to collect as many responses as is reasonable in the time available. Another option might be to ask parents to write down students' postassessment responses at home or during Expo.

Bee-Bots. We recommend that each classroom have access to 6–8 Bee-Bots. This is enough to support two learning centers, each with 3–4 Bee-Bots. Depending on class size and how the rotation through centers is managed, students may need to share and use the Bee-Bots in pairs. The Bee-Bot center should be directly supervised by the instructor; see "Teaching Bee-Bots" in the Teacher Preparation section for specific concepts to teach. If there are enough Bee-Bots available, you could also provide a Bee-Bot Free Play center where students have the freedom to use the Bee-Bots however they please and experiment with their own ideas.

Robot Mice and Code-a-pillar. Although Bee-Bots are the primary devices used in this course, students benefit from the opportunity to compare the Bee-Bots to other kinds of tangible tech devices. The Code & Go Robot Mouse and the Fisher-Price Think & Learn Code-a-pillar work well for challenging students to compare and contrast different types of devices and how they are programmed. (See "Compare Bee-Bots to Other Robots" in the Teacher Preparation Section.) Note that the Robot Mouse is small enough to use on a tabletop, but the Code-a-pillar requires a large floor space.

Construction. This center should be stocked with construction materials such as blocks, cardboard, and Straws and Connectors. Students can be challenged to build houses, fences, and other features of the Bee-Bot town. Rulers, pencils, and paper can also be used to facilitate and expand student explorations of size and scale as they build. Questions such as "How do you know if this house will be big enough for the Bee-Bots?" can help inspire students to incorporate measurement activities into their construction projects.

Clay robots. In this activity, students build their own robots out of clay or dough and use hardware to add features to their robots. Making clay robots is a safe way for students to enjoy a sensory experience with authentic robotics components. You will need soft clay or dough and hardware, such as nuts, bolts, washers, wire, or bottle caps. Place hardware on a tray or in paper plates and invite students to incorporate the metal pieces into their clay robots. Often, students will use the hardware to create faces and other features on their robots. This activity will challenge them to further explore the essential question "What is a robot?" Building robots out of clay and hardware also explores questions, such as "What is the structure (shape and form) of a robot?" and "What are the parts of a robot?"

Drafting. This center should be stocked with a variety of drawing and drafting tools, such as pencils, pens, markers, rulers, stencils, plain paper, lined paper, and graph paper. Students should be encouraged to use their time at the drawing and drafting center to explore making designs and plans for the Bee-Bot town, creating stories about bees or robots, or writing codes using symbols, letters, or numerals. Suggested tasks could include drawing a Bee-Bot house or mapping a Bee-Bot road. Instructor suggestions should follow the interests of students as the plans for the Bee-Bot town develop. For example, "Where will we place our traffic lights? Make a drawing that shows your ideas." Or, "Make a map that shows me how far the Bee-Bots need to travel to get to school."

Games. The two suggested games for this course are The Great Cheese Chase and Race to the Treasure! Both of these games are chosen to align with the spatial reasoning concepts in this course.

TEACHER PREPARATION

Teaching Bee-Bots and Programming Languages

Teaching students how to program a Bee-Bot to accomplish increasingly complex tasks will provide a foundation of programming knowledge and skills in the area of computer science. Here is a description of suggested programming tasks, from the most simple to the more complex. You may find that there are other interesting tasks that will engage students in even more exciting learning experiences.

1. **Meet the Bee-Bots: How to use the command buttons.** Initially, students will be eager to try out the Bee-Bots without waiting for instructions, which is fine. Once they've had a chance to experiment, there will be natural and spontaneous opportunities to clarify and introduce the functions of each button or command. Briefly demonstrate and explain to students the use of each of the direction buttons, the go button, the pause button, and the reset button. To teach the direction buttons, use

consistent language to name each direction—forward, back, right, left. Some young students may not yet have a clear understanding of right and left. You may need to incorporate that concept into the introductory lessons.

▸ **Teach the vocabulary for *symbol*, *code*, and *sequence*:** Use simple and direct language to describe and define these concepts. A symbol is something that stands for something else, like a smiley face means happy. An arrow pointing forward is a symbol for moving forward. A code is what you create when you put symbols in a row, on paper or when you program a Bee-Bot. A sequence is a bunch of symbols or commands in a row, in a particular order, one after another, on a page of paper or in time.

▸ **Spatial reasoning: Navigating on a grid.** In order to program a Bee-Bot to move from point A to point B, you have to reason or think about the path the Bee-Bot will take and translate that into a sequence of commands, or code. Students will need to predict, estimate, or measure distances in order to create their codes. One of the challenges most students will find is that a command to turn will only turn; it will not move the Bee-Bot forward. Students will learn through experimentation, trial, and error, that turning and moving are two separate commands. One way to add complexity to this process is to put new obstacles in the path of the Bee-Bot and challenge students to program the Bee-Bot to navigate around the obstacles.

2. **How can we represent our code?** Students will likely understand easily the idea that the arrow buttons on the back of the Bee-Bot control the actions of the Bee-Bot, but they will soon discover that it is hard to remember which buttons they have pushed. They will need a way to document or represent the code they are using to program the Bee-Bot. Explain to students that people communicate with robots through *computer code*. The creation of these codes is called *programming*. Codes can be written or recorded in many different ways. Each is a language.

▸ Every time students find a new way to represent their code, they have invented a new programming language. Use the closing circle at the end of each class session to share and demonstrate the different kinds of programming languages students have created and used each day. Challenge students to come up with their own way of representing the code, their own programming language. Perhaps they will discover that sound can also be used as a programming language (a tap means go forward, a stomp means go back). Some of the programming languages students can create and explore include:

- drawing arrows on index cards, each card representing a push of a button on the Bee-Bot's back, and lining up the cards in the row to create a *sequence* or *code*;
- drawing arrows or symbols on a long strip of paper or on a grid;
- creating a sequence of hand signals to represent the commands in the code; and
- stringing colored beads, each color of bead representing a command—green for forward, red for back, purple for right, orange for left.

3. **Synchronization:** The topic of synchronization will come up if students try to make multiple Bee-Bots race or dance together. Teach students the term *synchronize* to describe how students are aligning the timing of the Bee-Bot programming. This issue may also come up if the class builds a large and complex town in which multiple Bee-Bots are traveling multiple paths at the same time. A Bee-Bot traffic jam is a great opportunity to teach students the concept of synchronization and challenge them to coordinate their programming of the Bee-Bots to avoid traffic jams.

4. **Calibration and measurement, and maps:** At some point, students will discover that the Bee-Bots are *calibrated*. Every time the forward button is pushed the Bee-Bot moves forward exactly the same distance. Students will be challenged to measure and document what that distance is and incorporate that knowledge into their coding. This should happen almost naturally as students explore what a Bee-Bot can do. Be ready to facilitate that process with materials, such as big pieces of paper, rulers, and yardsticks, that can be used to document and measure the distances the Bee-Bots travel.

5. **Compare Bee-Bots to other robots:** Introduce one or both of these supplemental robots: the Code & Go Robot Mouse or the Code-a-pillar. The Code & Go Mouse is very similar to the Bee-Bot, and the similarities will be pretty clear to students. The biggest difference is that the mouse has a red button, which is a "random" command. This command is intended to add an element of chance to the programming of the robot. Students may enjoy the challenge of guessing what the red button means, or they may find that adding the element of chance to a logical programming process is odd and potentially frustrating. Discuss these observations and reactions with students. The Code-a-pillar is a fun, tangible tech tool. To minimize distractions in the classroom, we recommend disabling the audio feature on the device, but the lights will indicate which command the Code-a-pillar is following. Note that you will need a much larger space to operate a Code-a-pillar than the Bee-Bots or Code & Go

Mouse. You may want to take the Code-a-pillar outdoors during recess and use it on a paved playground surface.

IDEAS FOR DIFFERENTIATION

The structure of the lessons, with opportunities to explore a variety of learning centers, is designed to allow students to learn and explore at their own pace. Students who need more time to master new ideas can be allowed to spend a longer amount of time in a learning center, or be allowed to make their own choice for which center to visit, as long as that strategy does not disrupt the rest of the classroom.

For students needing greater challenge, here are some suggestions:

> **Programming languages:** Challenge advanced students to come up with programming languages that are completely different from those used in class. For example, a student who plays a musical instrument could create a piece of music in which specific notes or sounds represent specific commands or codes.

> **Mapping:** Students with advanced spatial reasoning skills could be challenged to create an accurate map of the Bee-Bot paths that the class has created or imagined. They could add advanced map features, such as a compass rose or a key to scale.

> **Documenting with words, images, audio, video:** A student who is reluctant to participate could be tasked with documenting the class's progress. He or she could write a story, take photos, or make a recording of the Bee-Bots and/or students. Students could also be challenged to write or dictate fiction about the Bee-Bots and what happens in their town.

> **Right angles and measuring angles:** A student with advanced math ability could be challenged to explore and measure the angles involved in Bee-Bot movements and programming. Each turn of the Bee-Bot is a "right" angle, which is 90 degrees. Introduce the student to the concept of angles and that angles can be measured by degrees. Ask: If a circle is 360 degrees, how many degrees is a right angle? How many degrees does the Bee-Bot travel if it turns right twice? A protractor could be introduced as a tool for measuring angles.

> **Critical thinking:** Challenge advanced students to think about how a Bee-Bot fits into the broader world of robots and computer programming. Ask: Is a Bee-Bot a toy or a robot? Why do you think so?

UNIT II
Robot Shortcut

COURSE DESCRIPTION

In the world of coding, a *function* is a shortcut that allows programmers to make their code more efficient or more elegant. In the world of robots, educational devices like the Primo Cubetto and KIBO robots teach students how to use a function command to help their robot friends take a shortcut on their way to fun adventures.

Essential Questions

> What makes a robot a robot?
> How do we write code that is "elegant"?
> What can we learn about computer programming from maps, games, and puzzles?

Learning Outcomes

During the course, students will:
> discuss and document the uses of coding terms such as *function* and *elegant code*;
> explore the design, mechanics, and programming of tangible tech devices, such as the Primo Cubetto and the KIBO robot;
> create increasingly complex and elegant codes to program robots to perform specific tasks and actions;
> use math and spatial reasoning skills to map and measure the paths of the robots; and
> compare and contrast the form and function of two kinds of robots, Primo and KIBO.

Materials

> Teacher's copies of read-aloud books (see Welcome Circle)
> Suggested videos (see Closing Circle)
> Student copies of Robotics Assessment (see p. 156)
> 1 Primo Cubetto Playset
> 1 KIBO Kit
> Extra batteries (AA)
> Paper, writing, and drawing materials for drafting
> Blocks, cardboard, or other construction materials
> Chutes and Ladders
> Parcheesi

LESSON PLANS AT A GLANCE

Monday	Tuesday	Wednesday	Thursday	Friday
Welcome Circle: Introductions and read *Me and My Robot*.	**Welcome Circle:** Read *As the Crow Flies*.	**Welcome Circle:** Read *Along a Long Road*.	**Welcome Circle:** Read *Katy and the Big Snow*.	**Welcome Circle:** Read *The Most Magnificent Thing*.
Mini-Lesson: Meet Primo Cubetto.	**Mini-Lesson:** Follow a Map.	**Mini-Lesson:** The function line.	**Mini-Lesson:** Compare Cubetto to KIBO.	**Mini-Lesson:** Troubleshooting.
Centers: 1. Preassessment 2. Cubetto 3. Drafting 4. Construction	**Centers:** 1. Cubetto 2. Games 3. Drafting 4. Construction	**Centers:** 1. Cubetto 2. Games 3. Drafting 4. Construction	**Centers:** 1. KIBO and Cubetto 2. Games 3. Drafting 4. Construction	**Centers:** 1. Postassessment 2. KIBO and Cubetto 3. Drafting 4. Construction
Recess/Break	**Recess/Break**	**Recess/Break**	**Recess/Break**	**Recess/Break**
Revisit Centers	**Revisit Centers**	**Revisit Centers**	**Revisit Centers**	**Prepare for Expo**
Closing Circle: Video clip.	**Closing Circle:** Video clip.	**Closing Circle:** Video clip.	**Closing Circle:** Video clip.	**Expo:** Display student work; students teach parents how to program Primo and KIBO.

LESSON DETAILS

Welcome Circle and Closing Circle

Welcome circle. Starting each class session with a welcome circle provides an opportunity to establish a sense of community, review the schedule and expectations, and take attendance. Students sit on the floor while the instructor leads the discussion. The instructor concludes the welcome circle with a read aloud of a storybook related to course concepts. Suggested books include:

> *Me and My Robot* **by Tracey West:** In this book, the conversations between the boy and his robot are a remarkably accurate demonstration of how a programmer might refine or troubleshoot his or her code to produce a desirable result. Discuss: What is a robot? How do we tell robots what to do?

> *As the Crow Flies: A First Book of Maps* **by Gail Hartman:** Use this book to inspire conversations about spatial reasoning. Discuss with students how they might create a similar story about Cubetto. Ask: Where does Cubetto go? What does Cubetto's map look like?

> *Along a Long Road* **by Frank Viva:** Like *As the Crow Flies*, this book can be used to talk about spatial reasoning in the context of programming a robot. Discuss: If this cyclist were a robot, what kinds of commands would you give him to make him visit these different places? Could you program Cubetto to do some of the things you see in this book? Could Cubetto go over a bridge? Can Cubetto speed up and slow down? Why or why not?

> *Katy and the Big Snow* **by Virginia Lee Burton:** This book also provides an opportunity to discuss maps and spatial reasoning. Discuss the route traveled by the snowplow, the landmarks visited along the way, and the different ways the maps and paths are represented in the book. Invite students to pretend that Cubetto is a snowplow, and have them create a program that will make Cubetto plow the roads in a pretend town.

> *The Most Magnificent Thing* **by Ashley Spires:** This book demonstrates a troubleshooting or problem-solving process. Discuss how the girl feels in the story. Ask: Do you ever feel frustrated when you are coding or making maps? What are some strategies you use to solve the problem?

Closing circle. At the end of each class, revisit one of the storybooks, reflect on student projects, or show and discuss a video clip about robots. Suggested videos include:

> "Inside the LEGO Factory: How Robots & Machines Make LEGO" (available at http://thekidshouldseethis.com/post/inside-the-lego-factory-the-robots-machines-that-make-lego)
> "KIBO Robot Group Dance" (available at https://www.youtube.com/watch?v=kxDWlcSnCL0)
> "The Next Generation of Boston Dynamics' Atlas Robot" (available at http://thekidshouldseethis.com/post/the-next-generation-of-boston-dynamics-atlas-robot)
> "A Robot Vehicle That Drives on Walls Using Propellers" (available at http://thekidshouldseethis.com/post/a-robot-vehicle-that-drives-on-walls-using-propellers)
> "Hop Aboard This Driverless Bus in Trikala, Greece" (available at http://thekidshouldseethis.com/post/hop-aboard-a-driverless-robotic-bus)

Mini-Lessons

See "Teaching Primo Cubetto, KIBO, and Programming Languages" in the Teacher Preparation section (p. 126) for information about how to introduce Primo Cubetto and teach specific concepts. Any large-group lessons should be brief. Students will have the opportunity to practice the concepts in learning centers.

Centers

Pre- and postassessment. The pre- and postassessments (see p. 156) are intended to measure and document students' general understanding of robots and computer programming. Students can draw or write their answers. The same handout can be used for both pre- and postassessment. Young students who are not fluent writers can be invited to dictate responses to an adult. In practice, it may be difficult to find classroom time for every student to dictate a response one-on-one with an adult. Instructors can try to collect as many responses as is reasonable in the time available. Another option might be to ask parents to write down students' postassessment responses at home or during Expo.

Cubetto. The Cubetto learning center should be set up in an area with enough floor space for the robot to roll at least 5–6 feet in any direction. The surface of the floor should be smooth and clear of obstacles. The instructor should be positioned at this center to introduce the robot to students and facilitate the introduction of new challenges. As described in the Teacher Preparation section, the Primo Cubetto set comes with a grid mat, but we recommend that instructors wait to introduce the grid until after students have had a chance to experiment with the robot and learn how to use the command blocks. Using an inquiry-based learning approach, students will often discover the need for a grid on their own and may enjoy creating their own mat, rather than using the preprinted mat.

KIBO. The KIBO robot provides an interesting contrast to the Cubetto robot. As described in the Teacher Preparation section, students can be challenged to analyze how the two robots are similar and how each is different and unique. Like the Cubetto robot, the KIBO learning center requires floor space for the robot to roll. The instructor will be needed to introduce the robot and help facilitate the activities. See the Teacher Preparation section for instructions for programming and operating the KIBO robot.

Drafting. This center is for different kinds of drawing, writing, drafting, and mapping activities. Instructors may suggest tasks or challenges to be addressed in this center, but students should also have the opportunity to choose their own tasks. The center should be equipped with different kinds of paper, writing and drawing materials, rulers, stencils, protractors, and examples of maps and algorithms. The materials can be rotated each day so there are always new materials or prompts to spark ideas.

Construction. The construction center is an open-ended learning center where students can experiment with construction materials and ideas that are related to the Primo and KIBO robots. For example, the center can be equipped with blocks, cardboard, or other construction materials. Students can be encouraged to create 3-D structures for the robots, such as bridges the robots can travel over or under, or homes that can house the robots. At some point, students will likely discover that they will need to measure the robots in order to create constructions that fit their size. Students can be encouraged to use both standard and nonstandard units of measurement. Have rulers, measuring tape, graph paper, pens, and pencils ready for students to document their ideas and research.

Games. The two suggested games for this course are Chutes and Ladders and Parcheesi. The instructions for each game are included in the box as well as online. Each game has some kind of shortcut built into the game, where a player can travel a significant distance forward or back with one move. As you play the games with students, talk about the ways these shortcuts are similar to a function line, loop, or other command used to program a robot.

TEACHER PREPARATION

Teaching Primo Cubetto, KIBO, and Programming Languages

Teaching students how to program a Primo Cubetto robot to follow increasingly complex paths will provide a foundation of programming knowledge and skills. Educator resources for Primo Cubetto are available at https://www.primo toys.com/education. Here is a brief description of suggested programming tasks, from the simple to the more complex. You may find that there are other interesting tasks that will engage students in even more exciting learning experiences.

1. **Meet Primo Cubetto: Programming basics.** Briefly demonstrate and explain the use of each of the direction pegs: forward, left, and right. Some young students may not yet have a clear understanding of right and left. You may need to incorporate that concept into the introductory lessons. Teach the vocabulary for *symbol*, *code*, *sequence*, and *algorithm*. Use simple and direct language to describe and define these concepts. A symbol is something that stands for something else, like a smiley face means happy. An arrow pointing forward is a symbol for moving forward. A code is what you create when you put symbols in a row, on paper or when you program a robot. A sequence is a bunch of symbols or commands in a row, one after another, on a page of paper or in time. An algorithm is a set of instructions.

2. **Follow a map:** Once students have learned the basic commands and how to use the command board, challenge students to navigate a specific path. In order to program Cubetto to move from point A to point B, you have to reason or think about the path the robot will take and translate that into a sequence of commands, or code. Students will need to predict, estimate, or measure distances in order to create their codes. One of the challenges most students will find is that a command to turn will only turn; it will not move the robot forward. Students will learn through experimentation, trial, and error, that turning and moving are two separate commands. One way to add complexity to this process is to put new obstacles in the path of the robot and challenge students to program the robot to navigate around the obstacles.

3. **Calibration:** At some point as students begin exploring what a robot can do, they will discover that the robots are *calibrated*. Every time the forward block is used, the robot moves forward exactly the same distance. Students will be challenged to measure and document what that distance is and incorporate that knowledge into their coding. This should happen

almost naturally as students explore what a robot can do. Be ready to facilitate that process with materials, such as big pieces of paper, rulers, and yardsticks, that can be used to document and measure the distances the robots travel.

4. **The function line or "shortcut":** Teach students to use a function command to create more "elegant" code. On the Cubetto pegboard, the commands placed in the function line can be represented by the light blue block. When the function block is placed in the sequence, students use one block to represent a set of commands in the function line, thereby creating a more elegant code. Discuss how the function line serves as a "shortcut" that allows the programmer to do more with less. Here is a video tutorial for introducing the function block: https://www.youtube.com/watch?v=wHx88dAghAU.

5. **Compare Cubetto to KIBO:** The KIBO robot is a tangible tech tool that teaches students how to program a robot by placing command blocks in a sequence. The robot has a scanner that reads the bar code on each block: http://resources.kinderlabrobotics.com/resource/creating-and-scanning-programs. After students have a chance to try both robots, discuss the interesting similarities and differences between Cubetto and KIBO, and, if time permits, create a Venn diagram recording students' observations.

6. **Troubleshooting:** Frustrations and problems are inevitable when working with robots and learning how to code. Use *The Most Magnificent Thing*, as well as real-life examples from class, to talk about how it feels when things don't go as planned and, most importantly, what strategies we can use to overcome obstacles.

IDEAS FOR DIFFERENTIATION

The structure of the lessons, with opportunities to explore a variety of learning centers, is designed to allow students to learn and explore at their own pace. Students who need more time to master new ideas can be allowed to spend a longer amount of time in a learning center, or be allowed to make their own choice for which center to visit, as long as that strategy does not disrupt the rest of the classroom.

For students needing greater challenge, here are some suggestions:

> **Programming languages:** Challenge advanced students to come up with programming languages that are completely different from those used in class. A student who plays a musical instrument could create a piece of music in which specific notes or sounds represent specific commands or codes.

> **Mapping:** Students with advanced spatial reasoning skills could be challenged to create accurate maps of the various paths students have created or imagined. They could add map features, such as a compass rose or a key to scale.

> **Documenting with words, images, audio, and video:** A student who is reluctant to participate could be tasked with documenting the class's progress. He or she could write a story, take photos, or make a recording of the robots and/or students. Students could also be challenged to write or dictate fiction about the robots, imagining their personalities and adventures.

> **Right angles and measuring angles:** A student with advanced math ability could be challenged to explore and measure the angles involved in robot movements and programming. Each turn of a robot is a right angle, which is 90 degrees. Introduce the student to the concept of angles and that angles can be measured by degrees. Ask: If a circle is 360 degrees, how many degrees is a right angle? How many degrees does the robot travel if it turns right twice? A protractor could be introduced as a tool for measuring angles.

> **Critical thinking:** Challenge advanced students to think about how the robots fit into the broader world of robots and computer programming. Ask: Which do you like better, the Primo or the KIBO? Why? How could you improve on the functioning or design of these robots? If you could build your own robot, what would it look like? How would you program it?

Use online resources for additional lesson plans and activity ideas. The resources on the Cubetto website (https://www.primotoys.com) and KIBO website (http://kinderlabrobotics.com) provide many additional lessons and activities that could be adapted to challenge a student or a group of students who are ready to consider more advanced robotics concepts.

UNIT III
Robot Reaction

COURSE DESCRIPTION

How do we tell robots what to do? We give them commands in the form of code. Some robots also have sensors that allow them to see, hear, or sense their environments. In this course, young robotic engineers learn to code educational robots like Ozobots and Hexbugs as they observe and analyze how sensors enhance a robot's functioning.

Essential Questions

> How does a robot know what to do?
> Can a robot think like a human?
> How does a robotic sensor work?

Learning Outcomes

During the course, students will:
> define and use computer programming terms and concepts, such as *code*, *algorithm*, and *troubleshooting*;
> explore the design, mechanics, and programming of robotic devices such as Hexbugs, Ozobots, and Cubelets;
> conduct experiments and research that demonstrate the purpose and function of robotic sensors; and
> collaborate with other students to create projects that explore the capacity of robots to sense and respond to their environment.

Materials

> Teacher's copies of read-aloud books (see Welcome Circle)
> Suggested videos (see Closing Circle)

> Student copies of Robotics Assessment (see p. 156)
> Hexbugs (recommended: Nanos, Scarabs, Ants, Larvae, AquaBots; 2–3 Hexbugs per center)
> 1–2 Ozobots
> 1–2 Cubelets
> Extra Hexbug batteries
> Broken Hexbug parts
> Small screwdrivers
> Ozobot markers (black, red, blue, green)
> LEGOs and blocks
> Walls & Warriors game
> Labyrinth game
> Paper, writing, and drawing materials for drafting

LESSON PLANS AT A GLANCE

Monday	Tuesday	Wednesday	Thursday	Friday
Welcome Circle: Read *If I Had a Robot.*	**Welcome Circle:** Read *Boy + Bot.*	**Welcome Circle:** Read *Me on the Map.*	**Welcome Circle:** Read *My Map Book.*	**Welcome Circle:** Read *My Truck Is Stuck!*
Mini-Lesson: Sensors.	**Mini-Lesson:** Ozobots.	**Mini-Lesson:** Cubelets.	**Mini-Lesson:** Compare Ozobot and Cubelet sensors.	**Mini-Lesson:** How smart is this robot?
Centers: 1. Preassessment 2. Hexbugs on land 3. Hexbugs at sea 4. Construction	**Centers:** 1. Ozobots 2. Hexbugs 3. Games or drafting 4. Construction	**Centers:** 1. Cubelets 2. Ozobots 3. Games or drafting 4. Construction	**Centers:** 1. Ozobots and cubelets side by side 2. Hexbugs 3. Games 4. Drafting	**Centers:** 1. Postassessment 2. Ozobots 3. Cubelets 4. Hexbugs
Recess/Break	**Recess/Break**	**Recess/Break**	**Recess/Break**	**Recess/Break**
Revisit Centers	**Revisit Centers**	**Revisit Centers**	**Revisit Centers**	**Prepare for Expo**
Closing Circle: Discuss video clip.	**Closing Circle:** Discuss video clip.	**Closing Circle:** Discuss video clip.	**Closing Circle:** Discuss video clip.	**Expo:** Display student work; students teach parents to build and program robots.

LESSON DETAILS

Welcome Circle and Closing Circle

Welcome circle. Starting each class session with a welcome circle provides an opportunity to establish a sense of community, review the schedule and expectations, and take attendance. Students sit on the floor while the instructor leads the discussion. The instructor concludes the welcome circle with a read aloud of a picture book that relates to course content. Suggested books include:

> *If I Had a Robot* **by Dan Yaccarino:** Discuss: What is a robot? How does a robot know what to do? What kind of robot do you wish you could have?

> *Boy + Bot* **by Ame Dyckman:** Discuss: How are people and robots the same? How are they different? Can a robot think like a human?

> *Me on the Map* **by Joan Sweeney:** Use this book to draw students' attention to the importance of mapping and spatial reasoning in programming a robot. You may want to mention that programming many robotic devices, like autonomous vehicles, requires the programmer to teach the robot how to navigate a map. Discuss: What might an Ozobot map look like? What might a Hexbug map look like? What does a programmer need to know about maps?

> *My Map Book* **by Sara Fanelli:** This map book demonstrates that there are many different ways to represent a map on paper. All maps use some kind of a system of symbols, such as lines, arrows, or a compass rose. Discuss: How is programming a robot like drawing a map?

> *My Truck Is Stuck!* **by Kevin Lewis:** This book demonstrates a troubleshooting or problem-solving process. Discuss the strategies that the characters in the book tried to solve the problem. Some were helpful and some were not. Ask: Do you ever feel frustrated and stuck when you are coding or making maps? What are some strategies you use to solve your problems?

Closing circle. At the end of each class, revisit one of the storybooks, reflect on student projects, or show and discuss a video clip about robots. Suggested videos include:

> "Hexbug Larva-How It Works" (available at https://www.youtube.com/watch?v=JIXQ_vlPdlQ)

> "Stanford's uTug Microrobots Can Pull a Car" (available at http://thekidshouldseethis.com/post/stanfords-%c2%b5tug-microrobots-can-pull-a-car)

> "ChainFORM, Robot Modules That Can Transform" (available at http://thekidshouldseethis.com/post/chainform-modules-by-mits-tangible-media-group)
> "Handle, Boston Dynamics' Robot on Wheels" (available at http://thekidshouldseethis.com/post/handle-boston-dynamics-robot-on-wheels)
> "Almost-Invisible Hydrogel Robots That Can Grab Quickly" (available at http://thekidshouldseethis.com/post/almost-invisible-hydrogel-robots-that-can-grab-quickly)

Mini-Lessons

See "Teaching Robots and Sensors" in the Teacher Preparation section (p. 134) for information about how to introduce the robotic devices and teach specific concepts. Any large-group lessons should be brief. Students will have the opportunity to practice the concepts in learning centers.

Centers

Pre- and postassessment. The pre- and postassessments (see p. 156) are intended to measure and document students' general understanding of robots and computer programming. Students can draw or write their answers. The same handout can be used for both pre- and postassessment. Young students who are not fluent writers can be invited to dictate responses to an adult. In practice, it may be difficult to find classroom time for every student to dictate a response one-on-one with an adult. Instructors can try to collect as many responses as is reasonable in the time available. Another option might be to ask parents to write down students' postassessment responses at home or during Expo.

Hexbugs on land and Hexbugs at sea. The classroom should be stocked with a variety of Hexbug devices to set up one center for walking (land) Hexbugs and one center for swimming (sea) Hexbugs. As students explore how the Hexbugs work, challenge them to observe the creatures as scientists, observing the behaviors and characteristics of these creatures. Ask students: How would you describe the overall size and shape of this Hexbug? How many legs or other features does it have? What do you notice about the design of this robot and the materials used? How was it built? How would you describe the movements of this Hexbug? Does it move fast or slow? What path does it follow? Have students document their ideas and observations on a chart or separate sheets of paper.

The term *bio-inspired robotics* is used to describe robots, such as Hexbugs, that simulate living organisms. Note that the term *bio-robotics* (or *biorobotics*, depending on your fondness for hyphens) has a different meaning—it is used most often in the field of medicine to describe research and programs that incorporate robotics to heal or help the human body. Hexbugs are actually closer to the family of *bio-inspired robotics* than *bio-robotics*. Background information about both *bio-robotics* and *bio-inspired robotics* can be found in the Resources section of this unit.

For the purposes of this course, students should be introduced to both terms, *bio-robotics* and *bio-inspired robotics*. We suggest explaining to students that *bio-robotics* is a field in medicine and health care and informs, for example, how an artificial hand might be designed. *Bio-inspired robotics* is a field in engineering and informs, for example, how a robotic rover might move across the surface of Mars.

As the course progresses through the week, some of Hexbugs will lose power or break. Use these events as teachable moments to talk about and explore the mechanical engineering of robot. Establish an area of the classroom for a Hexbug hospital or a Hexbug morgue. Provide screwdrivers and extra batteries. Students can work on reviving these Hexbugs with new batteries or they can conduct autopsies by taking apart the "dead" Hexbugs.

Construction. The construction center should be stocked with construction materials that will allow for open-ended exploration, such as LEGOs and blocks. Hexbugs can also be incorporated into construction. For example, students could build Hexbug Nano mazes out of LEGOs (see Robot Reactions Resources for video examples).

Ozobot and Cubelets. The Ozobot robot and the Cubelets building set are two examples of educational devices that incorporate sensors into their design. Any device with a sensor could be used in combination with the Hexbugs to challenge students to observe and experiment with the ways robots respond to their environment. We recommend that instructors add one learning center devoted to Ozobot play on the second day of class and add one learning center devoted to Cubelets on the third day of class. Then, on the fourth day of class, these two devices could be used side by side and students can be challenged to compare the two devices through instructor-facilitated discussion, through student journaling, by creating a Venn diagram, or any combination of these strategies. Details and links for learning to use these devices can be found in the "Teaching Robots and Sensors" section.

Games. The two suggested games for this course are Walls & Warriors and Labyrinth. These games have been selected to align with the spatial reasoning and logic skills involved in programming robots. The instructions for each game are included in the box as well as online.

> Walls & Warriors: http://www.smartgames.eu/en/smartgames/walls-warriors. This game is described as a single-player game, but in this class, the game could be used cooperatively with a pair of students.

> Labyrinth: https://www.ravensburger.com/uk/games/family-games/ labyrinth/index.html

Drafting. One center can be set aside for different kinds of drawing, writing, drafting, and mapping activities. Instructors may suggest tasks or challenges to be addressed in this center, but students should also have the opportunity to choose their own tasks. The center should be equipped with different kinds of paper, writing and drawing materials, rulers, stencils, protractors, and examples of maps and algorithms. The materials can be rotated each day so there are always new materials or prompts to spark ideas.

TEACHER PREPARATION

Teaching Robots and Sensors

Introduce the concept of sensors to students by asking them to identify human senses. People can see, hear, touch, smell, and taste. Can a robot see and hear? How? For background information on robot sensors, visit http://www. robotplatform.com/knowledge/sensors/types_of_robot_sensors.html.

Some Hexbugs have sensors and some do not. When students are experimenting with the Hexbugs in the learning centers, challenge them to try to figure out which Hexbugs have sensors, what kind of sensors they are (touch, light, movement?), and how the sensors work. For example, the Hexbug AquaBot has pressure sensors on its sides. When there is even pressure on each side, such as when the device is submerged in water, the sensor activates the motor and the AquaBot begins to swim.

The Ozobot has color sensors that allow it to read the colors on the page. The Ozobot kit comes with a set of templates that can be used to demonstrate and test the Ozobot. If time permits, students can also use markers to draw roads and patterns for the Ozobot to follow. Use the Ozobot teacher guide or one of the other "quick start" resources to find out how to introduce the Ozobot to students: http://ozobot.com/stem-education/education-getting-started. A hard copy of the Quick Start Guide is included in the kit.

Cubelets are another kind of robotic device that uses sensors. One of the simplest constructions is the "Dud Light," a three-block structure that includes the battery cube (power), the brightness cube (senses light), and the flashlight cube. When students visit the Cubelets learning center, they can build the Dud Light and test it out by dimming the available light under a cloth. Students who enjoy the challenge of building with Cubelets can be invited to build other structures. For quick tips on how to get started, visit http://www.modrobotics.com/cubelets/cubelets-getting-started. More information about using Cubelets is available online and on the package inserts.

Challenge students to think critically about the similarities and differences between the sensors in the Ozobot and the Cubelet sensors. You can also include Hexbug sensors in the conversation. If time permits, create a Venn diagram documenting student observations and discoveries.

As the course concludes, challenge students to think deeply about how robots with sensors might be used outside of the classroom. What are the opportunities and benefits of using robots in our world—for entertainment, transportation, industry, health care? What are the limitations of robots? Are there things that people can do that robots will probably never be able to do? Invite students to include their thoughts and ideas in their work on the postassessment.

IDEAS FOR DIFFERENTIATION

The structure of the lessons, with opportunities to explore a variety of learning centers, is designed to allow students to learn and explore at their own pace. Students who need more time to master new ideas can be allowed to spend a longer amount of time in a learning center, or be allowed to make their own choice for which center to visit, as long as that strategy does not disrupt the rest of the classroom.

For students needing greater challenge, here are some suggestions:

> **Documenting with words, images, audio, and video:** A student who is reluctant to participate could be tasked with documenting the class's progress. He or she could write a story, take photos, or make a recording of the Hexbugs, Ozobots, Cubelets, and/or students.

> **Build and program with Cubelets:** Students needing an additional challenge can be invited to experiment with the Cubelets. The set of Cubelet blocks can be used to create structures or "robots" from the very simple to the very complex. They are also compatible with LEGOs, so many design features can be built onto the cubes with LEGOs. See the Cubelets website for more information.

> **Hack the Hexbugs:** Students needing an additional challenge can also be encouraged to "hack" the design of the Hexbugs to create their own kind of creature. Lightweight materials such as wire and paper can be attached to a Hexbug to alter the appearance and the movements of the Hexbug.

> **Evaluate the Hexbugs:** Students with a lot of experience and prior knowledge about Hexbugs can be encouraged to create their own Hexbug

design and send their ideas and feedback to the Hexbug company using the contact information found on the website.

> **Explore Ozobot:** Students with an interest in drawing may particularly enjoy creating roads and patterns with the Ozobot markers. Ideas for teachers can be found on the Ozobot website at http://ozobot.com/stem-education.

ROBOTIC REACTION RESOURCES

> Hexbug (available at https://www.hexbug.com)
> Cubelets Education (available at http://www.modrobotics.com/education)
> Bio-inspired robotics resources:
  ▸ Wyss Institute: Autonomous Flying Microbots (RoboBees) (available at https://wyss.harvard.edu/technology/autonomous-flying-microbots-robobees)
  ▸ Bio-inspired robotics video (available at https://vimeo.com/15739182)
  ▸ "Bugs and Bots Enthrall at Ed Portal" (available at http://www.thecrimson.com/article/2011/2/4/finio-kids-bugs-robots)
  ▸ "Channeling Your Inner Entomologist" (available at http://static.nsta.org/files/sc1409_28.pdf)
  ▸ "Hexbugs-Robot Toys Mimic Animals" (available at http://singularityhub.com/2009/09/23/hexbugs-robot-toys-mimic-animals-videos)
  ▸ Festo BionicANTs (available at https://www.festo.com/group/en/cms/10157.htm)

> Video resources:
  ▸ "The Sticky Wonder of Gecko Feet" (available at https://www.ted.com/talks/robert_full_on_animal_movement)
  ▸ "3-D X-ray Provides Detailed Images of How Living Insects Move" (available at https://www.youtube.com/watch?v=sGsbUDwO1F4)
  ▸ Insects and animals in slow motion:
    - "Walking Ant in Slow-Motion" (available at https://www.youtube.com/watch?v=IHEYBvriv2I)
    - "Insect Flight in Slow Motion" (available at https://www.youtube.com/watch?v=DlF91R41Pso)
    - "Fastest Animals on Earth in Slow Motion-Animal Camera-BBC" (available at https://www.youtube.com/watch?v=zcWxAfl0okE)

- ▶ Hexbug mazes:
    - – "LEGO Hexbug Maze With 5 Hexbugs" (available at https://www.youtube.com/watch?v=lVnUWDv5S7g)
    - – "LEGO Maze for Hex Bug Nano 2010" (available at https://www.youtube.com/watch?v=7j5VnM6375M)
    - – "Hex Bug LEGO Maze" (available at https://www.youtube.com/watch?v=4DXYsw_uD4U)

- ▶ "Can a Hex Bug Fish Swim in the Sea??? Aquabot Swimming Test Review Micro Robotic Robot" (available at https://www.youtube.com/watch?v=HFd1vDe8cwc)
- ▶ "Can a Hex Bug Fish Swim in Chocolate Syrup?? Aquabot Swimming Test Review Micro Robotic Robot" (available at https://www.youtube.com/watch?v=4ag7DWwrQks)

- > Picture books related to hexbugs, insects, machines, toys, or bio-robotics
    - ▶ *The Beautiful Beetle Book* by Sue Unstead (Nonfiction, lift-the-flap book)
    - ▶ *Bug Off!: Creepy Crawly Poems* by Jane Yolen (Praying Mantis on pp. 8–9 looks like a robotic arm)
    - ▶ *Bugs A to Z* by Scholastic (Nonfiction reference book)
    - ▶ *Cockroach* by Karen Hartley
    - ▶ *Color and Noise!: Let's Play With Toys!* by Janice Lobb
    - ▶ *Creepy, Crawly Jokes About Spiders and Other Bugs* by Melissa Stewart
    - ▶ *Eight Legs Up* by David Kirk (How the number of your legs affects what you can do well)
    - ▶ *Flit, Flutter, Fly!* edited by Lee Bennett Hopkins
    - ▶ *The Foot Book* by Dr. Seuss (Whimsical look at all different kinds of feet)
    - ▶ *How Toys Spin* by Helen Whittaker
    - ▶ *Insect Bodies*, A Bobbie Kalman Book (Nonfiction, looks at backbones, body sections, eyes, antennae, legs, wings)
    - ▶ *Leo Cockroach, Toy Tester* by Kevin O'Malley
    - ▶ *The Magic School Bus Explores the World of Bugs*
    - ▶ *Making Things Move* by Dustyn Roberts
    - ▶ *Martina the Beautiful Cockroach* by Carmen Agra Deedy
    - ▶ *Miss Spider's Tea Party* by David Kirk (Rhyming picture book about a spider and her insect friends)
    - ▶ *Nasty Bugs: Poems* edited by Lee Bennett Hopkins
    - ▶ *Pull, Lift, and Lower: A Book About Pulleys* by Michael Dahl (Nonfiction, simple machines)

- *Roadbuilders* by B. G. Hennessy (Beautifully illustrated picture book about the big machines that make roads)
- *Simple Machines* by Allan Fowler
- *Simple Machines* by Rebecca Rissman
- *Swimmy* by Leo Lionni

UNIT IV
Robot Games

COURSE DESCRIPTION

Exciting new tangible devices like Sphero, Blue-Bot, and Bloxels allow students to learn about both coding and robotic engineering. This course introduces coding, engineering, and spatial reasoning concepts as well as game design. Students use robotic and coding tools to create games that demonstrate design elements, such as victory conditions. Although this course is designed for children in second grade, these lesson plans also include options for differentiation that allow for scaffolding for third graders.

Essential Questions

> What do computer scientists need to know to build and program robots?
> How can we use robots and code to create and play games?
> What are the differences and similarities between digital games and real games?

Learning Outcomes

During the course, students will:
> engage in critical thinking and discussions to determine a collaborative definition of the term *robot*;
> learn to program a robot using visual and block programming languages;
> collaborate with students to create and play games using tangible tech devices, computer code, and traditional game materials; and
> evaluate and improve game designs using a design engineering process.

Materials

> Teacher's copies of read-aloud books (see Welcome Circle)
> Suggested videos (see Closing Circle)

> Student copies of Robotics Assessment (see p. 156)
> Blue-Bot, programming tray, and chargers
> Sphero
> Bloxels Starter Kit
> 4–6 iPads with Sphero and Bloxels apps
> Latice game
> Gravity Maze game
> Code Monkey Island game
> Qwirkle game
> Rubik's cubes
> Game pieces, cards, dice, etc. for making games
> LEGOs
> Paper, writing, and drawing materials for drafting

LESSON PLANS AT A GLANCE

Monday	Tuesday	Wednesday	Thursday	Friday
Welcome Circle: Introductions and read *Me and My Robot*.	**Welcome Circle:** Read *The Bot that Scott Built*.	**Welcome Circle:** Read *Robot Zot!*	**Welcome Circle:** Read *Robo-Sauce*.	**Welcome Circle:** Revisit picture books: "Which book most accurately represents real robots?"
Mini-Lesson: Meet Blue-Bot.	**Mini-Lesson:** Meet Sphero.	**Mini-Lesson:** Creating Bloxel games.	**Mini-Lesson:** What makes a game a game?	**Mini-Lesson:** How can we combine the robots together to make a cool game to show our families at EXPO?
Centers: 1. Preassessment 2. Blue-Bot 3. Games 4. Construction	**Centers:** 1. Sphero 2. Blue-Bot 3. Drafting center 4. Games	**Centers:** 1. Bloxels 2. Blue-Bot 3. Sphero 4. Make your own game	**Centers:** 1. Blue-Bot 2. Sphero 3. Bloxels 4. Drafting 5. Games	**Centers:** 1. Blue-Bot 2. Sphero 3. Bloxels 4. Drafting 5. Games
Recess/Break	**Recess/Break**	**Recess/Break**	**Recess/Break**	**Recess/Break**
Revisit Centers	**Revisit Centers**	**Revisit Centers**	**Revisit Centers**	**Prepare for Expo**
Closing Circle: Video clip.	**Closing Circle:** Video clip.	**Closing Circle:** Video clip.	**Closing Circle:** Video clip.	**Expo:** Present class story; display robots; students teach parents how to program using block programming.

LESSON DETAILS

Welcome Circle and Closing Circle

Welcome circle. Starting each class session with a welcome circle provides an opportunity to establish a sense of community, review the schedule and expectations, and take attendance. Students sit on the floor while the instructor leads the discussion. The instructor concludes the welcome circle with a read aloud of a storybook that relates to the topic of robots. On the last day of class, challenge students to evaluate the books in response to the question "Which book most accurately represents real robots?" Suggested books include:

> *Me and My Robot* **by Tracey West:** In this book, the conversations between the boy and his robot are a remarkably accurate demonstration of how a programmer might refine or troubleshoot his code to produce a desirable result. Discuss: What is a robot? How do we tell robots what to do? This book could also be used to discuss the concept of *machine learning*, how an artificially intelligent machine takes in new information and uses it to make decisions.

> *The Bot That Scott Built* **by Kim Norman:** Discuss: Could someone your age really build a robot for a science fair? Why or why not? If you had a chance to program this robot, what would you make it do?

> *Robot Zot!* **by Jon Scieszka:** In this story, a robot comes in contact with other machines. Ask students to think about the differences between robots and other machines they know. Discuss: How is a toaster like a robot? How is a television like robot? How are they different?

> *Robo-Sauce* **by Adam Rubin:** Discuss: Could a person really turn into a robot? Would you ever want a robot dog for a pet? In real life, can a robot be evil? Can it be good?

Closing circle. At the end of each class, revisit one of the storybooks, reflect on student projects, or show and discuss a video clip about robots. Suggested videos include:

> "Madeline the Robot Tamer & Mimus" (available at http://thekid shouldseethis.com/post/madeline-the-robot-tamer-mimus)

> "How BB-8—a Rolling Robot in a Galaxy Far, Far Away—Changed Everything for Sphero" (available at https://www.wired.com/2015/12/how-bb-8a-rolling-robot-in-a-galaxy-far-far-awaychanged-everything-for-sphero)

> "Building a Volcano-Bot: How She Works" (available at http://thekid shouldseethis.com/post/building-a-volcano-bot-how-she-works)

> "Robots Trailer" (available at http://movies.nationalgeographic.com/movies/robots)
> "Virginia Tech: Autonomous Robotic Jellyfish" (available at https://vimeo.com/62880818)

Mini-Lessons

See "Teaching Blue-Bot and Sphero" and "Teaching Bloxels and Games" in the Teacher Preparation section (p. 143) for information about how to introduce the robotic devices and teach specific concepts. Any large-group lessons should be brief. Students will have the opportunity to practice the concepts in learning centers.

Centers

Pre- and postassessment. The pre- and postassessments (see p. 156) are intended to measure and document students' general understanding of robots and computer programming. Students can draw or write their answers. The same handout can be used for both pre- and postassessment. Young students who are not fluent writers can be invited to dictate responses to an adult. In practice, it may be difficult to find classroom time for every student to dictate a response one-on-one with an adult. Instructors can try to collect as many responses as is reasonable in the time available. Another option might be to ask parents to write down students' postassessment responses at home or during Expo.

Devices: Blue-Bot, Sphero, and Bloxels. Over the first 3 days of this course, students are introduced to three different types of programmable devices with three very different kinds of interfaces. The Blue-Bot is programmed by putting command cards/tiles in a tray. The Sphero is programmed using a touchscreen on a tablet. The Bloxels games are created by placing colored cubes onto a grid. Details, resources, and instructions for using these devices can be found in the Teacher Preparation section. Instructors will likely need to introduce each new device to students in each center and help facilitate any troubleshooting along the way. The physical space needed for each of these devices varies. Although the Bloxels kit can be used at a table or desk, the Blue-Bot and Sphero should be used on the floor. The Sphero, in particular, is able to move quickly over a large area. If a large space is not available, students can be given the challenge of programming the Sphero to stay within a small defined space. If your classroom has access to more than one Blue-Bot or Sphero, we recommend using one at a time, as the wireless signals between devices can get crossed when multiple devices are used in the same classroom.

Games. The suggested games for this course include Latice, Gravity Maze, Code Monkey Island, and Rubik's cubes. Each of these games is very different from the others. The variety is intended to spark discussion about the many different structures and elements that can be included in game design, both digital and tangible. Another option for this center is to invite students to create their own board game.

> Latice: http://www.latice.com
> Gravity Maze: http://www.thinkfun.com/products/gravity-maze
> Code Monkey Island: http://codemonkeyplanet.com
> Rubik's Cubes: https://www.rubiks.com

Construction. The construction center can be a place for open-ended construction with LEGOs or a place to build accessories, obstacles, or homes for the robots. Have students sketch or take photos of the designs they create.

Drafting. During center time, one center should be set aside for different kinds of drawing, writing, drafting, and mapping activities. Instructors may suggest tasks or challenges to be addressed in this center, but students should also have the opportunity to choose their own tasks to work. The center should be equipped with different kinds of paper, writing and drawing materials, rulers, stencils, protractors, and examples of maps and algorithms. The materials can be rotated each day so there are new materials or prompts to spark ideas and make connections between the open-ended activities and the robotics and coding concepts.

TEACHER PREPARATION

Teaching Blue-Bot and Sphero

Blue-Bot is a tangible tech robot that can be programmed two ways—by manipulating the buttons on the back of the device or through a wireless connection with a TacTile Reader Tray (https://www.bee-bot.us/bee-bot/accessories/tactile-reader.html). User guides for the bot and the tray are included with each device. Initially, allow students to experiment with the robot and the tray in an open-ended manner using trial and error. Once they begin to see what the bot can do, challenge them to program the bot to follow increasingly more complex patterns and paths.

Sphero SPRK is a rolling robot that can be programmed two ways—through a simple visual programming interface or through a more complex programming language that resembles Scratch (https://edu.sphero.com/cwists/preview/1671x).

An iPad with the Sphero Lightning Lab app is required to operate the Sphero. A hard copy of the Quick Start Guide is included in the box with the robot. Once the app is open, follow the "Connect Robot" prompts to activate the wireless connection between the tablet and the robot. The simple visual programming interface is called "Drive." Using this interface, students can control the Sphero by moving their finger on the touchscreen.

Here are some Sphero tutorial videos:
> "Sphero Spark Edition Basic Set Up" (available at https://www.youtube.com/watch?v=zTDST2nBaBc)
> "What Is Sphero SPRK Edition?" (available at https://www.youtube.com/watch?v=Yg8LmEkI_0c)
> "Sphero SPRK Unboxing and Demo" (available at https://www.youtube.com/watch?v=JK-pBYX-JDk)

Teaching Bloxels and Games

Bloxels is a digital game creator that combines hands-on tangible building with a game design app. The app allows students to take a photo of the block design they built and incorporate that tangible design into their digital game. A Bloxels tutorial video is available at https://www.youtube.com/watch?v=YhVBdN-2Vr8.

What makes a game a game? Discuss the elements of game design that make a game fun, challenging, and engaging. Ask students to describe the digital and tangible games that they enjoy, and create a class list of the elements students describe and identify. Elements may include mystery, action, challenge, risk, chance, space, goals, components, mechanics, rules, conflict, cooperation/competition, strategy, and/or victory conditions. Encourage students to observe, create, and incorporate these elements into their work with the robots and the other projects in the course. For background information about game structure, resources include:
> "Eight Game Elements to Make Learning More Intriguing" (available at https://www.td.org/Publications/Blogs/Learning-Technologies-Blog/2014/03/Eight-Game-Elements-to-Make-Learning-More-Intriguing)
> "Learning Game Design: Game Elements" (available at http://www.theknowledgeguru.com/learning-game-design-game-elements)

IDEAS FOR DIFFERENTIATION

The structure of the lessons, with opportunities to explore a variety of learning centers, is designed to allow students to learn and explore at their own pace. Students who need more time to master new ideas can be allowed to spend a longer amount of time in a learning center, or be allowed to make their own choice for which center to visit, as long as that strategy does not disrupt the rest of the classroom.

For students needing greater challenge, here are some suggestions:

> **Blue-Bot:** The Blue-Bot tray includes a packet of extension cards that will allow students to create longer, more complex codes (available at https://www.bee-bot.us/extension-pack.html).

> **Sphero:** For students needing an additional coding challenge, invite students to begin learning the block programming included in the Sphero Lightning Lab app. When you open the programming section of the app, you'll see a bar menu along the bottom of the screen that shows the many different categories in the program. Most students will be adequately challenged to learn the Actions commands, but more advanced students can explore the other categories, which include controls, operators, comparators, sensors, events, variables, and functions.

> **Game design challenges:** For some students, the most interesting challenges will involve game design. If laptops or desktop computers are available for your class, some web-based resources for digital game design include:

  ▶ Blockly Games (available at https://blockly-games.appspot.com)

  ▶ Code.org game design challenges:

  – Flappy Bird (available at https://studio.code.org/flappy/1)

  – Minecraft (available at https://code.org/Minecraft)

  ▶ Sploder! (available at http://www.sploder.com)

Teacher Preparation

DISPOSITIONS AND SKILLS FOR TEACHING TECH

Although no prior tech experience is required to teach Tech Beginnings courses, certain teaching dispositions are beneficial, such as a curiosity about how things work and an interest in inquiry-led learning. Instructors must be willing to experiment and take risks, modeling problem-solving and troubleshooting strategies as they learn alongside students.

In terms of classroom management, teachers should be familiar with how to implement a learning center structure. This includes the ability to set up the centers in the classroom as well as managing the transitions and rotations between the centers. Teachers must be willing to set clear expectations for the use of materials, especially fragile tech devices, and create a classroom environment where group work, collaboration, and conflict resolution are highly valued.

CORE CODING CONCEPTS

For both the coding and the robotics courses, the teacher should be familiar with some core computer science concepts. The term *coding* is often used broadly to mean all things related to computers, but coding is actually a specific task. To code, or to write code, means to program a computer or robot. The code is the message that tells the computer or robot what to do. Many are familiar with the term *code* as related to secret codes or Morse code. A code is a sequence of symbols, such as letters or numbers, that represent meaning. Coding in computer science is an active process in which the programmer makes decisions about what to accomplish and then writes or creates a code to make that happen.

The educational coding apps used in the courses use visual programming languages in the form of block code. The blocks of code often look like building blocks, colorful rectangles or shapes like puzzle pieces. Each block is labeled with an icon or text that indicates the purpose of the command. It's important for instructors to understand that when students use block code, there's also code behind the code. A programmer has built the blocks of code using another programming language, such as Python or Java, programming languages that are made up of more complex combinations of text, numerals, and other symbols. There's even code behind the Python and Java code: binary code, which is made up of zeros and ones. Just as a living cell is comprised of molecules, and molecules are comprised of atoms, a block of code is comprised of smaller and more complex parts. This big idea of coding is important in guiding students to a broad, universal understanding of the core structures and concepts in computer science.

ESSENTIAL CONCEPTS

A good source of introductory coding is Code.org. The Hour of Code tutorials are an excellent first coding experience for both children and adults: https://code.org/learn. Code.org also provides teacher resources available at https://code.org/educate.

Additionally, the K–12 Computer Science Framework website and downloadable documents also provide an overview of core computer science concepts as well as helpful resources: https://k12cs.org.

Here is a list of key terms and concepts included in the units:

Code: A system of symbols for communication; in computer science, a code is a set of instructions written in a programming language.

Sequence: A particular order of events or things, one following another.

Symbol: An image, mark, or character that represents an object, process, or idea.

Pattern: A combination of objects, symbols, actions, or events that form a consistent arrangement; recognizing and creating patterns is an important part of the coding process.

Command: An order given by a programmer to a computer or robot.

Algorithm: A set of step-by-step instructions for completing a task.

Loop: A programming structure that repeats a sequence of instructions.

Conditions: A feature of a programming language that directs the computer to follow the coded instructions based on whether certain criteria are met; conditions may be described using the words *if* and *then*.

Function: In computer programming, a procedure or routine that has been created and stored for later use.

MAKING ROBOTICS MEANINGFUL

To teach the robotics units, teachers will need to familiarize themselves with the instructions for each device. Additionally, teachers are encouraged to reflect upon which activities and strategies in the robotics units their particular students, with their own unique interests and abilities, will find most meaningful. Some students will be drawn to robots simply by the novelty of the devices, but students will be more likely to engage in a deep learning process when they find the topic personally meaningful.

Each of the robotics units follows a similar sequence of challenges:

> inquiry-based learning (how does it work?);
> intentional programming (challenge to get from A to B);
> navigating a grid;
> calibration and measurement;
> synchronization;
> storytelling; and
> problem solving.

Throughout the units, the curriculum text and structures encourage conversations about what role robots can and should play in our lives. How can robots help make the world a better place? The curriculum uses strategies, such as storytelling and games, to help engage students in explorations of meaning. In addition to the coding and engineering concepts, the curriculum also touches on what it means to be good digital citizens. Having holistic and open-ended conversations about computer science when children are young will ultimately help them understand and improve the world in which we live and prepare them for a technologically advanced future that we can't yet imagine. The young children in our classrooms today may someday figure out how technological tools can help keep people healthy, protect the environment, or make other important changes and improvements. As educators, our role is to empower students to be innovators and creators, not passive consumers of whatever new tech gadgets come along.

Assessment

PRE- AND POSTASSESSMENTS

Most of the Tech Beginnings units suggest the core pre- and postassessments. The pre- and postassessments should be completed on the first and last day of class, respectively. These assessments should collect information about students' understanding of broad concepts related to computers, tablets, code, and computer programming. The handouts for these assessments are included at the end of this section, and Figure 6 includes examples of completed assessments.

Note that the instructions within the units suggest drawing and dictation as alternatives for young students who are not able to read or write fluently. A few of the units, such as Hexbug Habitats and WeDo Go, suggest assessment activities that are specific to the unique tools and concepts addressed in that unit. See the lesson plans for details.

ASSESSMENT OPTIONS IN THE CODING APPS

Additionally, many of the apps, such as Kodable, ScratchJr, and Hopscotch, provide options for assessment as part of the app design or as resources online, such as the ScratchJr "Circle the Blocks" assessment tool.

Instructors can also save projects and screenshots that can be used to develop a digital portfolio of student work. For example, students can "save" their creations in ScratchJr as "projects." Instructors should develop a system for naming the projects so they have a record of which students worked on which proj-

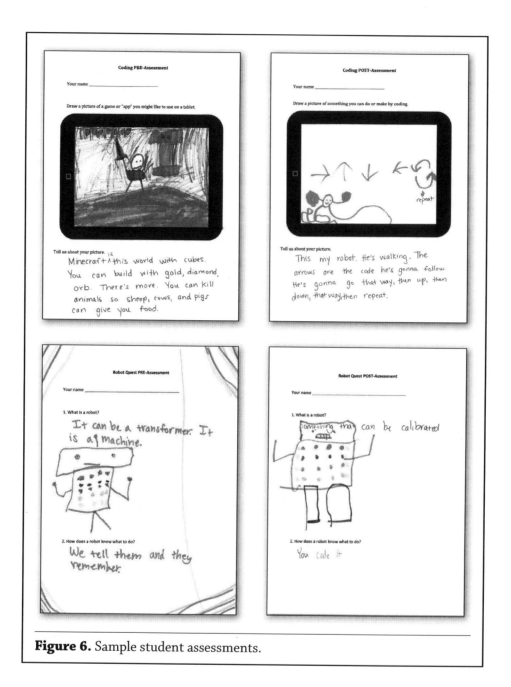

Figure 6. Sample student assessments.

ects. Instructors can take a screenshot on an iPad at any time during a student's project or game using the following method: https://support.apple.com/en-us/HT200289. The screenshot will be saved as a photo in the Photos app. Later, the photo can be e-mailed as an attachment to your own computer.

A ScratchJr project can be exported and e-mailed using the e-mail function within ScratchJr. However, the person receiving the e-mail must open it on an iPad with ScratchJr. It can't be opened and viewed on a device that does not have a ScratchJr app. Also, some iPads used by schools require special settings in order to authorize or unlock the tablet to allow the sending of e-mails.

COLLECT OTHER DOCUMENTATION OF STUDENT LEARNING

Instructors can observe and write anecdotal notes, take student dictation of stories and conversations, take digital photographs throughout the learning process, and collect or copy student work. All of these sources of information will be helpful for student assessment.

CODING PREASSESSMENT

Directions: Draw a picture of a game or "app" you might like to use on a tablet.

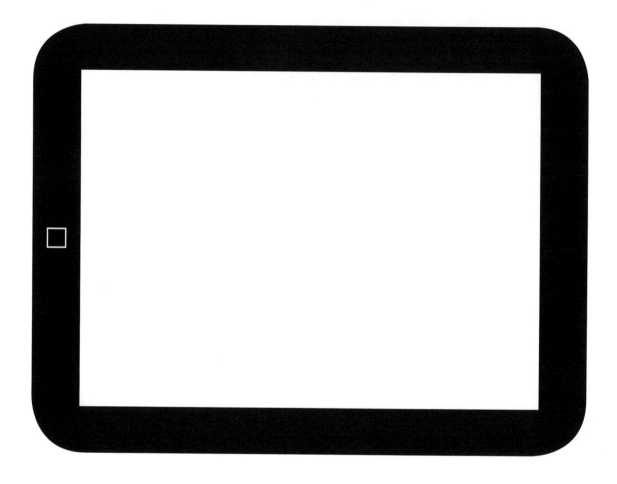

Tell us about your picture.

_____

_____

_____

_____

_____

Name:_____ Date:_____

CODING POSTASSESSMENT

Directions: Draw a picture of something you can do or make by coding.

Tell us about your picture.

_____

_____

_____

_____

_____

ROBOTICS ASSESSMENT

Directions: Answer the following questions using what you know about robots. You may write, draw, or dictate your response.

1. What is a robot?

2. How does a robot know what to do?

Materials and Equipment

This section details the apps and devices used in the Tech Beginnings curriculum.

APPS

All of the recommended apps in the lesson plans are available on iPads. Most, but not all, are also available on Android tablets. A full-size tablet is recommended. For implementing most units, a collection of four to six tablets is enough for the class. Students will rotate through the centers, and for a class size of 15–24 students, only four to six will be using the device center at a time.

These apps are intended for use by beginners of all ages. Most are icon-based and require very little reading of text.

Daisy the Dinosaur
http://www.daisythedinosaur.com

This free app is available only for iPads at this time through the Apple App Store. The app was created by Hopscotch Technologies. A review of the app is available at https://www.commonsensemedia.org/app-reviews/daisy-the-dinosaur.

Kodable
https://www.kodable.com

The initial download of Kodable is free (iPad only), but there are additional levels of games that must be purchased. One of the nice features of the free version of Kodable is a learning guide for parents and teachers about the coding concepts that are embedded in the game.

ScratchJr

https://www.scratchjr.org

ScratchJr is a free educational app that allows the user to create and animate characters. Instructors may benefit from having access to copies of *The Official ScratchJr Book* (https://www.amazon.com/Official-ScratchJr-Book-Help-Learn/dp/1593276710). There are also ScratchJr guides, lesson plans, and teacher information available at https://www.scratchjr.org/teach.

Hopscotch

https://www.gethopscotch.com

Hopscotch is free animation app that is similar to ScratchJr, but Hopscotch also includes an online community where users can share projects. Hopscotch includes commands, tools, and features that lend themselves well to game design. A curriculum guide is available for download here: http://hopscotch-curriculum-files.s3.amazonaws.com/Hopscotch_Curriculum.pdf.

Lightbot

http://lightbot.com/resources.html

The standard Lightbot app must be purchased, but there is a free "Hour of Code" version. The free version is fine for the Tech Beginnings units.

Toca Builders

https://tocaboca.com/app/toca-builders

Toca Builders is a commercial world-building app similar to Minecraft but tailored for a younger audience. The app allows the user to build a virtual world out of cube blocks by programming a group of robots, each with a unique structure and ability, to move and build.

Bloxels Starter Kit

http://www.bloxelsbuilder.com

Bloxels is a digital game creator that combines hands-on tangible building with a game design app. The app allows students to take a photo of a block design they build using small colored blocks in a frame and then incorporate that tangible design into their digital game.

DEVICES AND ROBOTIC KITS

The devices and robotic kits recommended in the Tech Beginnings units have been tested and evaluated by the CTD program staff. Currently, new robotics devices are frequently appearing on the market. The lesson plans are intended to be flexible enough to allow for substitution of different robotic devices, depending on what is available at each school. Cost, durability, and ease of use are among many of the considerations when considering which devices to purchase.

Bee-Bots

https://www.bee-bot.us

Bee-Bots are educational robots designed to introduce young children to computer programming. The Bee-Bots and many of the other recommended devices robots are called "tangible tech" because they are standalone programmable devices. You don't need a computer or tablet to use them. Students don't need to interact with a laptop or tablet screen, manipulate a mouse, or use a computer keyboard to tell the robots what to do. They tell the robot what to do by pushing buttons. Each push of a button or section of the chain is a command. The commands make up a sequence, and that sequence becomes the code. In this way, children learn to program a robot.

Blue-Bots

https://www.bee-bot.us/bluebot.html

Blue-Bots are very similar to Bee-Bots but also have the option of Bluetooth wireless programming using an app on a tablet or a TacTile Reader Tray.

Code-a-pillar

http://fisher-price.mattel.com/shop/en-us/fp/think-learn/think-learn-code-a-pillar-dkt39

Children program the Code-a-pillar to perform a sequence of commands by attaching segments to the base of the toy insect. Each segment represents a specific action or sound, as represented by an icon on the back of each segment. To minimize distractions in the classroom, we recommend disabling the audio feature on this device.

Code & Go Robot Mouse

https://www.learningresources.com/product/learning+essentials--8482-+programmable+robot+mouse.do

The Code & Go Robot Mouse is very similar to the Bee-Bot in design but smaller. It can be used on a tabletop rather than the floor.

Primo Cubetto

https://www.primotoys.com/education

The Primo Cubetto playset includes one wheeled robot, a pegboard, an assortment of colored programming pegs/blocks, and a mat. Children program the robot by placing a sequence of blocks in the queue on the programming board.

This set is more costly than many of the other recommended devices used in the Tech Beginnings curriculum, but the Primo sets are very well designed and offer interesting features, such as the function line, that are not available in other sets. Primo Cubetto resources and video tutorials are available at https://www.primo toys.com/resources.

KIBO
http://kinderlabrobotics.com/kibo

The KIBO robot was one of the first tangible tech devices to become available to educators. The basic KIBO 10 kit is enough to implement this Tech Beginnings curriculum, although the larger kits, with sensors and additional command blocks, provide more options for differentiation. The Kinderlab team at Tufts continues to develop curricula and teacher materials that support the use of this device. KIBO resources are available at http://resources.kinderlabrobotics.com, and curricula are available at http://kinderlabrobotics.com/curricula.

Hexbugs
https://www.hexbug.com

Hexbugs are popular robotic toys that come in many different models, from the tiny Nano cockroach to the remote-controlled Spider. The design and movements of these bio-inspired robots are remarkably similar to the real living creatures. In addition to the small mechanical bugs, the Hexbug company also sells educational robotic kits called Vex. The Vex kits require more advanced robotics and programming knowledge than the Hexbug activities described in these lesson plans.

Ozobot
http://ozobot.com/stem-education

The Ozobot robot is a small rolling robot equipped with sensors that read the lines and colors on paper. Students learn to program the Ozobot using templates and stickers provided with the robot or by drawing their own Ozobot codes and paths.

Cubelets
http://www.modrobotics.com/education

Cubelets are small magnetic blocks that snap together. Each block is designed to perform some kind of robotic function: Some have battery power, some have wheels or lights, and some are equipped with sensors. Students build robotic structures according to suggested combinations, or they can experiment and create their own designs

Sphero

https://store.sphero.com/products/sprk-plus

Sphero is a rolling ball-shaped robot that is programmed using an app on a tablet or smartphone. The app provides multiple interfaces for programming the robot to move, from an very easy beginning mode to more complex block coding options.

LEGO WeDo

https://education.lego.com/en-us/shop/view-all-products?product_lines=WeDo

LEGO robotics kits have been widely used in schools for many years. Both the WeDo and the EV3 Mindstorms kits continue to be the gold standard for introducing students to the combination of both the building and the programming of robots. For this unit, we recommend the WeDo 2.0 Core Set.

Resources

WEBSITES

Blockly games
https://blockly-games.appspot.com
These online games help teach block programming. Some reading is required.

Code.org
https://code.org
Code.org is a global nonprofit organization with a mission to expand participation in computer science classes and learning activities. The website and resources are constantly expanding. The "Hour of Code" campaign and materials are a great way to introduce adults and students to programming. The tutorials for beginners at Level 1 include many games and activities that would be appropriate for young students. These are web-based games played online on a computer, laptop, or tablet.

Common Sense Media
https://www.commonsensemedia.org
A great resource for reviews of all kinds of media, including movies, digital games, and apps.

DevTech Research Group at Tufts
http://ase.tufts.edu/devtech
The DevTech group first developed the technology used in KIBO robots and continues to be on the cutting edge of tangible tech.

Google: Made w/ Code

https://www.madewithcode.com

This website is a clearinghouse for projects, challenges, and tutorials intended to engage children and youth in learning to code. There is a focus on encouraging girls and young women, but the projects are appropriate for any gender.

Hour of Code

https://hourofcode.com/us/learn

Popular characters from movies and mass media like *Moana*, *Star Wars*, and *Frozen* are featured in fun, accessible tutorials that are created to introduce computer science concepts to beginners. These tutorials are also helpful for parents and teachers to learn basic coding concepts.

K–12 Computer Science Framework

https://k12cs.org

This overview of computer science concepts and practices organized by grade levels includes an excellent summary of relevant computer science concepts and approaches for early childhood classrooms.

Kodable

https://www.kodable.com

The initial download of Kodable is free (iPad only), but there are additional levels of games that must be purchased. One of the nice features of the free version of Kodable is a learning guide for parents and teachers about the coding concepts that are embedded in the game.

National Association for the Education of Young Children and Fred Rogers Center for Early Learning and Children's Media at Saint Vincent College Position Statement

http://www.naeyc.org/files/naeyc/file/positions/PS_technology_WEB2.pdf

The National Association for the Education of Young Children revised this position in 2012, expanding its view of the positive potential for the role of technology and digital media in the lives of young children.

Technology in Early Childhood Center of the Erikson Institute

http://teccenter.erikson.edu

The TEC center is a hub of resources for early educators to help them make appropriate decisions about the role of technology in the lives of young children.

BOOKS

Dinosaur-Themed Picture Books

Dinosaurs, Dinosaurs by Byron Barton
Dinosaur Roar! by Paul and Henrietta Stickland
Edwina, the Dinosaur Who Didn't Know She Was Extinct by Mo Willems
Goldilocks and the Three Dinosaurs by Mo Willems
How Do Dinosaurs . . . Series by Jane Yolen
If the Dinosaurs Came Back by Bernard Most

Picture Books That Can Be Used to Demonstrate Various Coding Concepts

Caps for Sale: A Tale of a Peddler, Some Monkeys and Their Monkey Business by Esphyr Slobodkina
Five Little Monkeys Jumping on the Bed by Eileen Christelow
Good Night, Gorilla by Peggy Rathmann
Harold and the Purple Crayon by Crockett Johnson
King Bidgood's in the Bathtub by Audrey Wood
The Little Mouse, the Red Ripe Strawberry, and the Big Hungry Bear by Audrey Wood
Monkey and Robot by Peter Catalanotto
Monkey With a Tool Belt by Chris Monroe
Monkey: A Trickster Tale From India by Gerald McDermott
One Monkey Too Many by Jackie French Koller

Picture Books That Demonstrate Problem Solving, Sequencing, and Conditions

The Doorbell Rang by Pat Hutchins
If You Give a Mouse a Cookie by Laura Joffe Numeroff
Jump, Frog, Jump! by Robert Kalan
King Bidgood's in the Bathtub by Audrey Wood
The Little Mouse, the Red Ripe Strawberry and the Big Hungry Bear by Audrey Wood
The Most Magnificent Thing by Ashley Spires
Mr. Gumpy's Outing by John Burningham
No Problem by Eileen Browne
Rolie Polie Olie by William Joyce
The Runaway Bunny by Margaret Wise Brown

Sheep in a Jeep by Nancy Shaw
Who Sank the Boat? by Pamela Allen

Monster-Themed Picture Books

The Book That Eats People by John Perry
Frankenstein Makes a Sandwich by Adam Rex
Go Away, Big Green Monster! by Ed Emberley
Goodnight Goon: A Petrifying Parody by Michael Rex
I Need My Monster by Amanda Noll
If You're a Monster and You Know It by Ed Emberley
Leonardo, the Terrible Monster by Mo Willems
Little Monsters by Jan Pienkowski
The Monster at the End of This Book by Jon Stone
Monster Mess! by Margery Cuyler
Monsters on Machines by Deb Lund
Monsters Don't Eat Broccoli by Barbara Jean Hicks
Monsters vs. Kittens by Dani Jones
There Was an Old Monster! by Rebecca Emberley
Where the Wild Things Are by Maurice Sendak

Map Picture Books

As the Crow Flies: A First Book of Maps by Gail Hartman
As the Roadrunner Runs: A First Book of Maps by Gail Hartman
Follow That Map!: A First Book of Mapping Skills by Scot Ritchie
Me on the Map by Joan Sweeney
My Map Book by Sara Fanelli
Road Builders by B. G. Hennessy

Robot Picture Books

Boy + Bot by Ame Dyckman
Clink by Kelly DiPucchio
Cookiebot!: A Harry and Horsie Adventure by Katie Van Camp
Hello, Robots! by Bob Staake
I Like Robots by Olga Kilicci
If I Had a Robot by Dan Yaccarino
If I Had a Robot Dog by Andrea Baruffi
Me and My Robot by Tracey West
The Most Magnificent Thing by Ashley Spires

My Robot (Green Light Readers) by Eve Bunting
Oh No! (Or How My Science Project Destroyed the World) by Marc Barnett
The Robot Alphabet by Amanda Baehr Fuller
The Robot and the Bluebird by David Lucas
The Robot Book by Heather Brown
Robots Everywhere by Denny Hebson
Robots at Home by Christine Zuchora-Walske
Robots, Robots Everywhere! by Sue Fliess
Robot Rumpus by Sean Taylor
Rosie Revere, Engineer by Andrea Beaty
Wodney Wat's Wobot by Helen Lester

Picture Books That Show Paths or Roads

Along a Long Road by Frank Viva
Fred and Ted's Road Trip by Peter Eastman
Hare and Tortoise by Alison Murray
Katy and the Big Snow by Virginia Lee Burton
Road Builders by B. G. Hennessy
Story Path by Kate Baker

Children's Books About Patterns

A-B-A-B-A: A Book of Pattern Play by Brian Cleary
Anno's Counting Book by Mitsumasa Anno
Mouse Shapes by Ellen Stoll Walsh
Pattern by Henry Arthur Pluckrose
Pattern Fish by Trudy Harris
Shapes, Shapes, Shapes by Tana Hoban
Ten Black Dots by Donald Crews

Map and Atlas Websites

World Atlas
http://www.worldatlas.com/aatlas/world.htm

National Geographic Maps
http://www.nationalgeographic.com/kids-world-atlas/maps.html

40 Maps that Explain the World
https://www.washingtonpost.com/news/worldviews/wp/2013/08/12/40-maps
-that-explain-the-world

Recommended Video

Robots, The History Channel, 2008.

References

Bruner, J. (2002). *Making stories: Law, literature, life.* Cambridge, MA: Harvard University Press.

K–12 Computer Science Framework Steering Committee. (2016). *K–12 computer science framework.* Retrieved from https://k12cs.org

National Association for the Education of Young Children, & Fred Rogers Center for Early Learning and Children's Media at Saint Vincent College. (2012). *Technology and interactive media as tools in early childhood programs serving children from birth through age 8* [Position statement]. Washington, DC: Authors. Retrieved from http://www.naeyc.org/files/naeyc/file/positions/PS_technology_WEB2.pdf

Papert, S. (1993). *Mindstorms: Children, computers, and powerful ideas* (2nd ed.). New York, NY: Basic Books.

Pila, S., Alade, F., Lauricella, A., Gadzikowski, A., Wartella, E., & Uttal, D. (2016). *Learning to code in the classroom.* Paper presented at the 2017 Society for Research in Development Biennial Meeting, Austin, TX.

Richtel, M. (2014). Reading, writing, arithmetic, and lately, coding. *The New York Times.* Retrieved from https://www.nytimes.com/2014/05/11/us/reading-writing-arithmetic-and-lately-coding.html

About the Author

Ann Gadzikowski serves as Early Childhood Coordinator for the Center for Talent Development at Northwestern University in Evanston, IL. She is the author of many books for teachers and parents, including *Robotics for Young Children: STEM Activities and Simple Coding* (Redleaf Press, 2017). Her website is http://anngadzikowski.com.